MW00912427

Lighting
the north

An Anthology of Feminism and Cultural
Diversity from Across the Nation

Co-authored by:

Ky-Lee Hanson | Charleyne Oulton | Karen Swyszcz
Shirin Ariff | Eldyka Simpson
Crystal Hardy Zongwe Binesikwe | Sasha Rose
Nadia Dedic | Angel Kibble

Featuring:

Mia Martina | Susan Musgrave | Miss Emily | Krysta Lee
Mlle Elizabeth Ann | Karla Smith | Steph Clark

GOLDEN BRICK ROAD
PUBLISHING HOUSE

Published in Canada, for Global Distribution by Golden Brick Road Publishing House. North American Distribution by IPG.

www.goldenbrickroad.pub | www.ipgbook.com

For more information email: kylee@gbrph.ca

ISBN: 9781988736747

To order additional copies of this book: orders@gbrph.ca

Contents

About the Authors

Lighting the North: An Anthology of Feminism and Cultural Diversity from Across the Nation is written by previously published and award winning writers, authors, and songwriters. The authors are eclectic in their heritage and communal in their stance for human rights.

Ky-Lee Hanson is a publishing, hospitality, and real estate entrepreneur; she is First Nations, Scottish, French-Canadian, and Inuit.

Charleyne Oulton is a member of the Royal Canadian Navy; she is Scottish and Prussian.

Crystal Hardy Zongwe Binesikwe is host of *Under the Same Stars* podcast, and *Zee's Place* on CILU Radio; she is Rocky Bay First Nation.

Eldyka Simpson is a healer and entrepreneur; she is French-Canadian, Ukranian, Polish, Russian, and Norwegian.

Karen Swyszcz is a social entrepreneur, blogger, group fitness instructor, and the *Bacon Bits 'n' Bytes* podcast host; she is Filipino, Chinese, and Spanish.

Sasha Rose is an assistant publisher, hospitality entrepreneur, and yoga teacher in training; she is Kwakiutl First Nations, French-Canadian, Chinese, and Scottish.

Shirin Ariff is an award winning author, poet, inspirational speaker, and a women's resiliency coach; she is Indian-Bengali.

Nadia Dedic is a plant-based, raw food chef and Member of the Raw Food Chef Alliance; she is of Czech heritage.

Angel Kibble is a trauma informed certified coach, and Canadian Army Veteran; she embraces her Dutch and Scottish heritage.

This book features short stories by:

Mia Martina is a multi-platinum recording artist and entrepreneur; she is Acadian, Columbian, and French.

Miss Emily is a multi-award-winning musician; she is German, Hessian, British, and Scandinavian.

Susan Musgrave is an award-winning author, and nominee of the Governor General's Literary Award for English-language fiction.

Krysta Lee is an actor, singer, coach, and crew member on the Canadian hit tv series *Workin Moms*; she is Italian, German, Irish, Indigenous, and French-Canadian.

Steph Clark is a personal branding and makeup artistry entrepreneur; she is French-Canadian, Jamaican, and Ska Nah Doht First Nations.

Mlle Elizabeth Ann is a highschool educator, and animal activist; she is Swiss, German, and French.

Karla Smith is a personal transformation coach; she is of heritage from Barbados and England.

They all are Canadian.

The authors share stories of searching for and expressing truth within history, culture, heritage, womanhood, and self. What are some forgotten cultures across Canada? Within birthing rights and a woman's intuition—does the medical system respect our human nature? Growing up multicultural in a Westernized world—does Canada actually embrace diversity? These are some questions the authors pose, as they also discuss being sheltered from the cultural history of others and exploring it for the first time—in adult years; all too common custody battles and divorce—yet (strangely) taboo that leave us in the dark about our rights within a system that is supposed to, but doesn't always, have the best interest of the child and family at heart; financial struggles of marginalized single or working moms and people of colour; stereotypes and unequal opportunities because of heritage or economic status; and talented and smart women working harder for the same positions as men in male dominated industries. What they all have in common is the knowing of self, but *that* wisdom being challenged in an unexpressed but all too familiar expectation to conform.

Introduction
Ky-Lee Hanson

Lighting the North illustrates the diverse search for identity and belonging of each woman, and the collective spirit she is building amongst her Northern sisters. In the land of the strong, many of us have felt weak—disconnected, fearful, and victimized—yet we remain courageous. In the land of the free, many of us have felt isolated—restricted, cautious, and unwelcome—yet we remain hopeful. *Lighting the North: An Anthology of Feminism and Cultural Diversity from Across the Nation* is a beacon of courage and hope for union in Canada. We believe this land can be the place of tolerance it strives to be, and we want to shed light on how we can be whole.

This book explores the learning and beauty of this land and the people that call it home, and also the stigmas we face in our nation. Across our land there is history, forgotten heritage among all cultures, and innovation; there are ways for our society to grow through honouring others without worry of losing our own customs, listening to wisdom, learning from the past, trusting in others, being open to change, and progressing together.

Collectively as authors, we've experienced societal abuse because of our gender, culture, or economic status—we share our experiences as we know in doing so, it will help others to feel less alone. Our voices give hope to others as we aim for an end to inequality. When on common ground, we have the opportunity to see eye-to-eye and make progress together. And, if we don't ever fully understand each other, we can hold space and be sympathetic to misfortunes to which we will never be exposed. We can do our part to protect others from experiencing abuse and pain. Our society witnesses misogyny, gender bias, the "Old Boy's Network," racism, prejudice, and inequality. Pain, fear, and (generational) trauma prevent us from connecting—and not only within the abused, but within the abusers. People have been taught hate and fear, and as creatures of habit, people repeat what they know. Systemic judgement of women and people of colour teaches stereotypes that pave the road we (are expected to) take.

We don't have to accept "this is just the way things are." We all want to feel safe; but we will never feel safe until everyone feels safe. Let's focus on comforting others and finding resolution. Let's bring back childlike acceptance, curiosity, and willingness to learn. Let's be okay with hearing the truth and progressing from it. Our stories bring light to situations, so they can be acknowledged, then healed and changed. Bringing light to situations is not an act of spreading hate, it is speaking our truth and the truth of many; it is providing a platform and holding space for that change to begin. This book is a gentle nudge at hard subjects; it is a response and an amplifier for social change. And, it is done in a beautiful, poetic, inquisitive way through personal storytelling to invite you to see social change through our lens.

We are here to make sure everyone has a platform they feel safe standing on. As much as we speak, the more we must listen; to start a constructive dialogue. That is the point of storytelling for social change. This is the point of collective work—to value all voices, and not only to say you do, but do it through your actions. As stories come forward of people not being heard or treated fairly, as hard as it is, those that *are* listening need to lead the transformation toward justice and safety.

When *one* voices concerns, *all* must listen.

What we commonly notice is when a person speaks up, but another quickly shifts the feelings expressed as an attack onto themself or onto their beliefs, this could be to manipulate and unfairly influence the situation. It can be called reactive abuse, which is one of the most common tactics abusers use—it is to shift blame for the abuse onto the victim.[1] It's a form of oppression, where the abuser will aim for the victim to feel guilt and shame about speaking out on an issue. This book explores how not only individuals execute abuse, but how social structures do. The (sometimes unconscious) aim of the abuser is to cause mental distress, shift and twist the narrative, and confuse the victim and witnesses—often by portraying a sense of righteousness with an aim to convince, delivered through being overly emotional, defensive, loud, constant, reactive, or boasting their authority, title, or label. They will use past praise and past successful milestones of the group, institution, society in an attempt to override any current uncomfortable feelings. They will overly express how their intentions are good, and how hurt and saddened they are

---

1   Meagan M, "Reactive Abuse; What It Is and Why Abusers Rely On It," BTSADV (website), posted January 28, 2019, https://breakthesilencedv.org/reactive-abuse-what-it-is-and-why-abusers-rely-on-it/

for people voicing their feelings. Sometimes we see complete disregard for people's concerns—followed by threats. In these cases, you may feel that it would have been *easier* if you said nothing at all—to submit to it. This happens within places of business, politics, and amongst communities, families, and friends.

In a healthy relationship people answer to respond, not to react. We communicate to express, to explore what we are feeling, to be heard, to learn, with the goal of making sure everyone is taken care of. This seems to be missing in much of the dialogue we are having as a nation. When victims try to speak to abusers, they are often shut down and belittled; labelled a troublemaker, and receive response through the use of double standards. The abuser is not ready to change, they can't see anywhere they are, or were, wrong. We see this commonly in small constant doses of gaslighting in our everyday media, online discussions, and during debate between different generations and cultures. People aren't listening to acknowledge and understand, they are *listening* to defend.

This book is a response to structural and societal abuse of all kinds, not a reaction. We have not felt we can express our individualism, nor speak up within systems (educational, medical, judicial, and even within local and online communities). Structural abuse (also called societal abuse) is sexual, emotional, or physical abuse that is imposed on an individual or group by a social or cultural system or authority. Structural abuse is indirect, and exploits the victim on an emotional, mental, and psychological level. It could manifest itself through any situation within a cultural or social framework. Currently in most countries, there is no formal law that has been formulated against structural abuse, protecting the victim from such abuse, and enabling him or her to approach the court for relevant justice.[2]

All categories of structural abuse involve the manipulative control of time, energy, focus, and connection between people, groups, and organisations, in the service of one side, and to the disservice of the other. The feminist theorist Sandra Harding coined the term *standpoint theory* to categorize epistemologies that emphasize women's knowledge. She argued that it is easy for those at the top of social hierarchies to lose sight of real human relations and the true nature of social reality, and thus miss critical questions about the social and natural world in their academic pursuits. In contrast, people at the bottom of social hierarchies have a unique standpoint that is a better starting point for scholarship. Although such people are often ignored, their marginalized positions actually make it easier for them to define important research questions and explain social and natural problems.[3] Segregation is the action or state of setting someone or something apart from other people or things. Segregation becomes a social norm because of "herd mentality." It is a yield to "per-

2   "Structural Abuse," Wikipedia, last edited April 28, 2020, https://en.wikipedia.org/wiki/Structural_abuse#:~:text=Structural%20abuse%20is%20the%20process,cannot%20reverse%20and%20cannot%20change; "Structural Abuse," Wikia.org (website), accessed July 15, 2020, https://abuse.wikia.org/wiki/Structural_abuse

3   Elizabeth Borland, "Standpoint Theory," Encyclopaedia Britannica (website), last updated May 13, 2020, https://www.britannica.com/topic/standpoint-theory

ceived group pressures" by publicly expressing whatever sentiment is in agreement with the norm, and shows how easily one's point of view can be altered by those around them. We see this happen in school cliques, the workplace, politics, within medical beliefs, media, religion, in radical groups, and in economic and racial landscapes. Women in the workforce can be blacklisted on rumours of being too difficult, or for being sexually promiscuous, or for *not* giving into sexual advances. People of colour, women, and those that live with less financial means experience segregation through inaccessibility of equal job opportunities and advancement, healthcare, and safety—it continues to be the norm.

Those that we follow (people and systems) do not always have our best interest at heart, power does not mean smarter, legal does not mean moral. We are known to be an accommodating and humble country, which *maybe* has translated into being passive and silent in many situations. We do not want to admit there is evil and wrong doing so we turn a blind eye to it. It is easier to fear than it is to understand; so we run away from it; we ignore it; we hope it goes away; and sometimes we defend it. But why? It is not in our nature to do so—natural law theory provides an interesting perspective:

> **"Natural law theory** is a legal theory that recognizes law and morality as deeply connected, if not one and the same. Morality relates to what is right and wrong and what is good and bad.

Natural law theorists believe that human laws are defined by morality, and not by an authority figure, like a king or a government. Therefore, we humans are guided by our human nature to figure out what the laws are, and to act in conformity with those laws.

The term 'natural law' is derived from the belief that human morality comes from nature. Everything in nature has a purpose, including humans. Our purpose, according to natural law theorists, is to live a good, happy life. Therefore, actions that work against that purpose—that is, actions that would prevent a fellow human from living a good, happy life—are considered 'unnatural', or 'immoral.'

Laws have a purpose too: to provide justice. From a natural law perspective, a law that doesn't provide justice (an unjust law) is considered 'not a law at all.' Therefore, a law that is flawed is one that no one should follow."[4]

There are many laws and social norms in our society that are flawed—causing disadvantage. The same could

---

4   "Natural Law Theory: Definitions, Ethics & Examples," Study.com (website), January 2, 2016, https://study.com/academy/lesson/natural-law-theory-definition-ethics-examples.html

be argued for leadership and systems. A flaw is not when a person is growing, no one knows all and no one is *perfect*. A flaw is a defect, a break, something unavoidable, and possibly unfixable. The solution is change. Because we are a generation that did not impose these laws or social norms, they are not flaws within us. They are scars. We can let them heal, but not if we keep cutting them open. Every negative act from bullying in the school yard, to the lies spread to ruin someone's career, to belittling someone's choice of career, birthing practice, or where they come from—and degrading their opinion or opportunites because of it, to allowing unjust systems to exist, to racial inequality, to rape, to murder. It all does not serve a purpose. Why, when, how, was it decided some people are better than others? A fellow author at Golden Brick Road Publishing House, Lori Williamson, says we are in the age of narcissism. People take from others, they go about their actions without consideration of anyone else—and often their acts are to gaslight or segregate others so there is less competition and more control available for themselves. There is a one-sided battle happening; there has been for a very long time.

In a discussion online about an uprising toward a "wellness community" that was accused of narcissistic behaviour, culturally appropriating indigenous traditions, and gaslighting their female members around sexual abuse, some tried to discredit the advocates for using the word "victim" when explaining the claims of the people in the community. This led to a discussion around the proper usage of victim vs. survivor, abused, or person. My reply was well received and was as follows—I share it here because I have used the word victim within this introduction to our book:

> "We **are** victims in the eyes of the abusers. From what I see, you are calling out a community that is looking to attract potential victims, and allowing abusers to walk amongst them. And is encouraging people to forgive their abuser without proper therapy, and blanketing that forgiveness is the answer to all (spiritual bypassing). Which translates to, an abuser is sitting beside you in this room, if they see you as a victim, you have to forgive what they do to you if they do it. And you have to forgive them for the pain they caused others (even if the abused person doesn't)."

I felt this mirrored many situations our authors have been privy to. We need to acknowledge how people experience, and how abusers premeditate and act out: gaslighting, prejudice, manipulation, grooming, and violence towards women, children, and BIPOC (Black, Indigenous, and People of Colour)—as well as how missions get derailed because instead of listening to the issue, people pick it apart and reactively place judgement. There is a blaring issue that needs to come to light—inequality of our perspectives based on our status. This is not historical, it is current within our society—across Canada and down to the small communities—even ones boasting themselves as "wellness" and "spiritual."

We speak on women's rights because of the very fact there *is* a women-specific rights movement. Women's rights are human rights, but women are marginalized to a degree that we *need* our own movement—and we have been *moving* for far too long. The same goes with movements promoting racial equality, and government, medical, and police reform. We have these movements because they are needed. We all have a social responsibility, some choose to not acknowledge this because their lives seem unaffected, they have privilege that they do not want to exercise to help others. "At least it is not me" are words never thought of by our authors. We feel it all and we are here now to share with you some of those feelings.

When inequality comes up in discussion, it's commonly said, "At least Canada isn't as bad as _____." Being the lesser of two evils is not an accomplishment, it is not something to be proud of. We are told women have rights in Canada and that we are proud to be multicultural. We want these things, we love these concepts, but because of these boasted statements, when we experience them as false and we speak on it, people have a hard time understanding why we have something to say at all. They may have heard all their lives that Canada is free, humble, safe, and diverse. Even though our experiences challenge this belief, they are warranted.

Words form statements, which hold so much power. They help us to identify what it means to be a woman, Canadian, human. It has been hard to voice experiences when we are constantly met with rebuttals or double standards. Sadly, what this does is shift or impede the narrative. It's not a solution-focused model without all involved acknowledging: change is constant and certain; emphasis should be on what is changeable and possible; and they must want to change. We need change in order to survive. We are at war with our collective self, mostly because of how each other differ in gender and appearance—and it doesn't make sense.

We need to consider that people who don't want social change are comfortable in a level of privilege. They can't be blamed for not wanting a life they enjoy to change—why would anyone want to change a system that provides them choice, safety, and respect? No one wants to take that away from anyone, we just want to see more people be able to access a comfortable life. This book is to end unspoken one-sided agreements women and people of colour find themselves in. A life of settling is choosing a life not meant for you. We aren't okay settling amongst expectations, stereotypes, or lifestyles that make us feel invalidated. No one is better than another because of their gender, economic status, credentials, or colour of their skin. There is only one of each of us, there is no comparison. We are women that have broken through stereotypes, accepted and stood up for ourselves, and continue to be the light in the world we want to see more of. This book amplifies the voices that celebrate and embrace diversity.

Lighting the North: An Anthology of Feminism and Cultural Diversity from Across the Nation shines on issues we need to see and pay attention to. All we need is more tolerance. It is within us all—let it shine. *"Tolerance is respect, acceptance and appreciation of the rich diversity of our world's cultures, our forms of expression and ways of being human."* -UNESCO, United Nations Educational, Scientific and Cultural Organization

KRYSTA LEE

Italian | German | Irish | Indigenous | French Canadian
www.KrystaLee.com
ig: @KrystaLee111 | fb: Krysta.Lee.Fanpage
li: @KrystaLee | t: Krysta_Lee
yt: www.YouTube.com/KrystaLee123
imdb: www.IMDB.me/KrystaLee

Northern Lights

There is grand beauty here in the north.
Lush lands blanket the earth with more secrets
and wisdom than one can comprehend.

There is a grander beauty that lies within the
diversity of its people who call this land home.
Some have walked these native paths since
ancient times—
Others have since arrived and are eager to
grow their roots deeply within our culture.

The true north has a unique way of embracing
and blending villages in unison.
From across the globe we gather here.

We plant our seeds, share our traditions, and
raise our families.

The unexplainable force that
binds us is infinite.
It weaves our tribes together with eternal
threads of love—
Love for our nation, love for one another, and
love for ourselves.

We are northern lightworkers . . .

Our spirits sing proudly with the whispers from
our ancestors.
Our hearts beat to the echo of the drums
played by souls passed.
Our bodies dance with the blood of many
generations who came before us.
Our children are the seedlings of our elders
from far and beyond.

We see in colour.
We welcome all shades.
We coexist with respect for mother nature.
We are the love and light of the north.

We are the Northern Lights.

Chapter One

GIRL NOTHING, GIRL EVERYTHING

"We don't realize we are different until someone points it out to us."

KY-LEE HANSON

Ky-Lee Hanson

First Nations | Inuit | Chinese | Scottish
English | French-Canadian

ig: @kylee.hanson.bosswoman | @gbrpublishing
@oneida.grand

Ky-Lee Hanson is First Nations / Canadian, a successful serial entrepreneur, a multiple award winning author and publisher, and an advocate for socio-economic human rights.

She is inquisitive, self-sufficient, and self-aware. Through her studies in sociology, and health sciences she actively seeks deeper understanding of human interactions, motives, and needs in hopes to amplify or provide new solutions to the world. Ky-Lee is optimistic but understands things for what they are. Being someone who can spot potential, one of the hardest things she learns over and over is: You can't help someone who doesn't want to help themselves.

Ky-Lee has a problem-solving mind, and found the true strength of life and her endless capabilities through a serious health battle in her late twenties. Ky-Lee took control and, over the years, mastered how to get her power back: mind, body, and soul. She has also faced much adversity, and success, as a female entrepreneur that is focused on the well-being of women and people of colour.

She owns Oneida Grand Centre in Iroquois, Ontario, and Golden Brick Road Publishing House. Her business expansions include tech, real estate, and a goal to start an organization to help fund and support entrepreneurs. She thrives on creating businesses and platforms that provide opportunities for others and that promote social change. Ky-Lee has an open-door policy she learned from her mom, a listening ear, and an opportunity to lock arms and take you down your Golden Brick Road.

C hocolate. Strawberry. Vanilla. Mom called my sisters and me, from oldest to youngest, darkest to lightest skin, and one could ponder if it had something to do with our personalities. Me, Ky-Lee, the eldest, with a sense of richness, a bittersweet outlook on most everything, reserved but bold—chocolate. Sukey, the middle, sharp and sweet, beautiful, and outdoorsy—strawberry. And Sasha, the baby, quiet and gentle, with creamy white skin and a hint of spice in her blue eyes—the only of the children and parents to have blue eyes—vanilla. Eskimo Ice Cream, (Native Ice cream, Indian Ice cream, Alaskan Ice Cream) is called Akutaq which is a Yup'ik word that means something mixed, or mix them together. Our father—First Nations, our mom—white. We were born and raised on the West Coast of Canada.

This is a story of love and divide within oneself.

Coming up in a mixed race household, as not only the eldest of three girls but the youngest to two (significantly) older, half, and completely white brothers—positioned me to also be the middle child—I learned quickly that there are many perspectives and many truths to the same situation; things might not always look as they are nor stay as they once were. I've played every role with none being definitive.

My father's mother remarried before I was born so I have never known my birth grandfather and growing up, my grandpa that I do know is a white man—I didn't even realize he was (specifically) white and not my birth grandfather until I was well on my way to being a preteen. Some of my First Nations relatives are not blended and then many are, some are blood related and some are adopted, while others are inlaws. As a child I didn't know society had such focus on physical and bloodline characteristics. Naively, or lovingly, it did not phase me. Family was family and I accepted things for what I was told and what I felt in my heart—these people were my family. Some people had really dark skin, some people had really light skin, everyone talked and dressed differently: some preferring small towns, some city folk, some with different accents, some rich and some not, a multi-cultural family on every possible level—and other members were very well blended, being some of all, open minded and unique—like me. *Wasn't this normal?*

As a kid I thought it was pretty cool to have First Nations blood, but it would take close to thirty years for me to feel and express that admiration again.

Although I grew up on the West Coast where many First Nations people live, there were very few at my school. So few people of colour that when it came time to play Spice Girls, I was always Scary Spice. And if you take a look at my author photo, you can gauge just how white my community must have been.

We don't realize we are different until someone points it out to us. It's always the worst being the last one to know. Being different isn't unfortunate, it just comes unexpectedly and with additional obstacles.

A lifetime ago, one of my great grandfathers was a Chief, as I understand, and the government of Canada at the time *encouraged* bands to relinquish their First Nations "Indian" status so they could have voting rights and work within the western society. A love for this country and welcoming prosperity into the family (the lighthearted story I was told, when it could very much have been out of dire need and force) created a divide from our culture, or more so a hole. This happened to my family. When my grandmother "married out of race" to a white man, that act of love would divide the children and grandchildren from gaining status later on. To simplify, I was raised white by a mixed race family. The government made it so I couldn't claim my First Nations heritage. I was to be white. Disappointingly, very little about our culture would ever be passed down to me. *As if someone or something prevented this knowledge from carrying on.* The imposed shame associated with being First Nations, the alcoholism and poverty, the residential schools, the removal of people and culture, the segregation, the police brutality and systemic racism, the pain . . . there is much, understandably, that ancestors and elders do not share with us when we are children. Into adulthood some of us seek it out but find much of it has been erased—stolen. This has been referred to as Native Invisibility, where people remain invisible to policymakers, funders, and the public . . . this is compounded by historical trauma—that is, "the long term, intergenerational impact of colonization, cultural suppression, and historical oppression of Indigenous peoples," which manifests as internalized and often unresolved grief.[1]

The first racial name I recall being labelled as is "Indian" and I do remember my family teaching me that Indians come from India, and Christopher Columbus got it wrong and just called us "Indians" and it stuck . . . I was in fact not Indian. I found this embarrassing from each side of myself. How could white people continue calling Indigenous people of this land—Indian, when it is wrong, not only for us but for the people of India? And I didn't understand why Indigenous people allowed it—I didn't know of all the violence we experienced in having our history erased. Does our history not matter? Don't people have concerns about being blatantly incorrect? Why does my school book teach me incorrect information . . . Life in Canada continued on. I was a White Indian girl, not from India. My family also has Eskimo bloodline. Let's fast forward to 1997-ish, I was finishing up elementary school when the world wanted to become a little more politically correct. Canada was catching up on their geography and deemed that it was no longer okay to call us: Indians. What *I* called myself was no longer politically correct. Shortly after, neither was Eskimo. It was now a racial term. We were now called Inuit.

My world would continue to change with our elementary school introducing mandatory Native Studies to the curriculum—BUT *only* for Native children . . . We were

---

1   NJJN. (n.d.). Retrieved July 15, 2020, from http://njjn.org/article/native-american-heritage-month-invisibility-and-resistance

taken out of our classes, and put into a small room where we learned about native heritages. Six of us, experiencing segregation from our peers. Now that we were physically removed from class, the students noticed we were different. We had a *special* class—because of our skin. To this day I can't understand why *all* children did not learn the ways of the land and its history. The majority only learned one version—the white version.

Now that I had lost most of my friends and was now a weird kid in a *special* class, I was subject to racial slurs from the people I once called childhood friends. As time went on, the labels would continue to change to Native Americans to First Nations Peoples and most recently to Indigenous. Needless to say, I was frustrated by all of this and wanted no part of it. When my father left us when I was fourteen, my First Nations side of the family became separated from my sisters and I. So, I dyed my hair store-box blonde and was a *new* person. A white person.

My teen years were like that of most: dramatic, unstable, fun, risky, and full of music, cars, parties, and friends. I had two close native friends that also had white moms. We all hung out with the white kids and we were just us, living through adolescence. We would sometimes talk about experiences of racism, stereotypes, and how we were made to feel different but I don't recall the sharing of heritage. We didn't know a lot about our culture and it didn't come up in our day to day lives. The places I grew up were typical medium to low income suburbs. Safe, small towns. There were a lot of native reserves, the reservations are areas of land owned by native bands. We were always told to stay off the reserves. I was curious and thought I would be accepted by my people, but I soon came to realize I wasn't "native enough." I was even *more* done with all of this. Being white *is* so much easier.

It was complicated to find my native heritage, all I could find were stories that seemed too evil to be true. I wanted a future where I could share my views and better the world, as a First Nations woman, I didn't see that as possible. There was no one but Pocahontas as a role model, and lucky for her a rich, powerful, white dude loved her. I was scared of the challenges and couldn't set myself up for failure. I'm white.

Society raised us to be ashamed of our dark skin, but as I grew I became ashamed of my whiteness. There was reconciliation needed within my soul. As I aged, I felt a lot of shame and unease . . . confusion, especially when I was asked about my background. Many Canadians have assumed I am from Eastern Europe, or of Ukrainian or Spanish descent before considering the very people that first lived on this land. I've been misunderstood without first having the opportunity to speak.

I visit that special class room I was sent to as a child frequently in my mind. Our teacher was a beautiful woman, and I remember finding her interesting; was it because she looked similar to me, or was it because of the story I sensed she wanted to tell—that I needed to hear. I sit in that small, narrow, and warm room in my mind, at the round table in a plastic dark-blue chair, with grey carpet, primary red, blue, and grey walls (modern for the late 90s), the ceiling vent is blasting hot air, with my hands in my lap, gazing down at a painting of an Orca and up to connect with her as she circles the table sharing culture with us—with a burning intention to make sure we feel important and safe. I don't know if I verbally say it or if she feels my questioning—Why aren't all the Canadian students learning this history? Am I welcomed as a Canadian? Why us? Am I different? Each time I question, I feel more of her story.

I've come to accept that everyone is a little bit confused and generally trying to do their best around this subject, and if not, they need others to lead by example so they too can gain awareness. I know that people can only be as good as they have been taught. I know that knowledge has been kept hidden. I've come to accept that the people of the world have a significant amount of healing and learning left to do so we can each gain undivided acceptance of ourselves and others, for the collective good.

Indigenious guidance has been sheltered, twisted, and silenced; people can't share their story from within a place of fear. Growing up in a changing environment with labels being put on me and stripped from me, being told that my *forced identity* is not politically correct, with a burning desire to be accepted and have a prosperous future, led me into a place of conforming to colonialism and feeling isolated. Eventually I felt there was nothing left to do but break free. I didn't know what that freedom would look like but intuition pulled me. With little care on labels and titles that would be placed on me, as I came to realize how institutionalized it all was, I decided it wasn't going to change me at a core level. Freedom was letting go of all that others placed onto me. Freedom would be learning my story and being in control of writing the rest of it. So that is what I set out to do.

To get to where I am now, which is a by-choice childless, mid 30s feminist and human rights advocate, a woman with a big (yet gentle) and beautiful (and effective) voice, that runs multiple ethical businesses, and is finding how to embrace all her cultures, I focused on my calling of making social impact and my interest in business. I have seen this grow into a passion for socio-economic rights.

In business and charitable work, it would not take long for me to have a label wake up call in this aspect of life. Apparently without money you can not be a *philanthropist*. I was gravitating toward this word. So, I was drawn to volunteering, writing, and sharing knowledge—activities I have done since my youth. I wouldn't let a label or lack of one tell me I can or can't be generous and help others. With no money and no university degree I was "unqualified" often for even entry level jobs. In the mid 2000s and early 2010s, that piece of paper still meant everything. Moving to Toronto amongst young peers that held these papers within a few short years of their highschool graduation, I found myself so far behind the curve that I was going to have to find another way to catch up. Growing up in BC, education and cost of living was so high, for many including me, it wasn't possible without a grant or family funding. There was a visible divide. Toronto, when I arrived, was noticeably different—a place where white people are statistically a minority compared to immigrants and second and third south asian generations; yet native people were few and far between. So many new cultures to learn about, and an abundance of educational options—however I had to work to live.

I took online courses through various universities and colleges and became a fanatic about learning! I worked and I learned. The amount of classes I have *willingly* taken would make seventeen year old me's head spin! Though, she would be so proud of where we are. A thirty-five-year-old with many self-acquired and self-appointed *titles*: entrepreneur, multi-business owner, multi-property owner, woman, author, publisher, budding philanthropist, community leader, helper, advocate, Kwakiutl First Nation, bosswoman, and so much more.

I decide who I am.

While starting in business, along with finding I was unqualified or unfunded for most of everything I wanted to pursue, I also found being female came with its ridiculous and stereotypical challenges. Interviews were based on appearance, and long term career stability for a woman would come only without children and working *four times* as hard as male counterparts. Gender inequality is very real, work place sexual harassment is very real. Being a young woman without financial means and trying to build a career felt like an uphill trek with no peak in sight, with boulders whizzing past—while white men got to take the chair lift. I witnessed abuse go without justice, I witnessed men receive breaks, special treatment, and promotions they did not deserve when women did not. I paid attention to tired industries, unethical businesses, and people that were flat out terrible at their jobs. I knew I was capable of being more, and it was going to be up to my self-belief and determination to prove it and inspire and make change for other women. This is where I questioned my mental difference: *Do other people not think like me? Why do people admire my willingness, doesn't everyone fight for what they want? Do I have a brain tumour? Does my brain work too quickly? Do I have ADHD—yes most likely—absolutely. What is my personality type?* I have also questioned my soul difference: *Do others feel like me? Do others want a better world?* And my emotional difference: *Are others sad like I am? Do they feel sadness for the world? Are people genuinely kind? Are they scared like me? Do they want better for all?*

It took me a decade of hustling at just above the bottom of the barrel workplaces, trying to make

greatness with very little, but somehow I was always surrounded by a strong amount of good. I have faced racism, sexism, ageism, judgement, and injustice; not having the financial means for a university degree, coming from a broken family, uprooting myself many times as a young woman and "being the new person" in the pursuit for better experiences. I experienced narcissistic abuse, theft, and bullying from women that were so called friends and associates, and society repeatedly breaking my heart, but there has always been light—a guide telling me it's happening because I'm strong enough for it: to handle it, learn from it, and fix it for others. In the darkest moments of my life, I knew there was more to the surface level of the experience because of how the wound I felt was deeper than me, I felt for the abused, for the entire world. This pain is not only mine. It happens to so many. This is a guide we all have within us, a nudge to see a larger picture, we just don't always listen to what it means. It is our inner child and Spirit, or Higher Power devising a plan for us to live our purpose. We come to earth with a childlike wonder that we never lose, it is only suppressed by confusion of what we are told to be or told we are from racial slurs, derogatory gender norms, career titles we don't want, wife or husband (in an unhappy marriage), to degrading names we are called: difficult, bitch, unprofessional, stupid, and fat. This kind of confusion blurs our identity and often results in the heartbreak of self-love; a pain that leads to a buried silence that acts out as trauma. It repeats. As humans we have repetitive natures: addictive personalities, habits, and schedules. If we are taught bad, we do bad; if we are taught good, we do good. If we experience shame, it clouds judgement of ourselves and others. If we can't love ourselves, we can't love others.

We are not responsible for the pain that is placed on us or the trauma that is a byproduct, but we are responsible for our healing and to stop the cycle. I'm here to leave things better than I found them—and that is my true identity—a fixer. But I've learned to stop being a fixer of all, and to fix without enabling. There is always a difference to learn, a line not to cross. My identity is to fix but through creation via restoration. Giving new life to stories, people, and objects is where I shine. I am not a mediator, I am an advocate. I see what needs to happen to make something better, and I'll show you the way or connect you with the person that can, and side by side we will all work together. Purpose is not a career, title, or label. Purpose is a feeling.

Our purpose is to BE, to be a being of good. Passing that onto others so they pass it on further. Holding space for people to grow while committing to learning and self-development so you can guide them further is a legacy stronger than any title. The only way we grow is through sharing. Sharing our stories writes a collaborative new chapter for society. The only way we learn is from knowledge that others have left before us. To help others find their identity and calling, each and everyone must practice being an open book with an open mind, and an open heart. Nothing is determined except our existence, the rest falls in between perspectives, and peace lies within union.

I am becoming whole by embracing all parts of me and choosing how I mend and fill the divides I feel and come across; I am becoming whole by writing my story the way I decide to experience it and by being who I decide to be. I've felt like "girl nothing" with no specific identity, and I learned to be "girl everything" by embracing all that I am, want to be, need to be, and can be. It is momentous to connect with yourself and know that you are on your golden path—deep down you know how to get there.

* * *

Continued Findings:

After writing this piece, I discovered alternative information on the usage of the label "Indian" when referring to the First People's of our land. "Columbus called the tribal people he met 'Indio,' from the Italian in dio, meaning 'in God.'"[2] -Russell Means.

Leading up to the year 2020, it was commonly said it would be the year of clarity—2020 vision. While this speech was given in 1980, forty years later, it is teaching us. This year is exposing information that we need to learn from to reconcile and move forward with new perspectives in an empowered and unionized way. There is more to uncover and we will do so together.

2   Means, R. (2011). Revolution and American Indians: "Marxism is as Alien to My Culture as Capitalism". Retrieved August 28, 2020, from https://www.filmsforaction.org/news/revolution-and-american-indians-marxism-is-as-alien-to-my-culture-as-capitalism

MIA MARTINA

Acadian | Columbian | French
ig: @princessmiamartina

Mia Martina has made a name for herself as a multi-platinum, international recording artist. Based in Toronto and Miami, she grew up in Saint-Ignace, New Brunswick and later attended Carleton University in Ottawa where she obtained a Masters degree in psychology. While there, she interned at CP Records, where she moved from office work to singing backup for artists on the label. She made her solo recording debut with the global smash "Stereo Love." The song was nominated for a Juno Award for Dance Recording of the Year in 2011. Soon after, Mia secured eight gold records, two platinum records, and dominated charts all over the world. Proving herself as more than just a singer-songwriter, Mia has been celebrated as a savvy business woman providing mentorship to young girls and businesswomen alike.

* * *

When I tell people that I grew up in a French village of only 500 people called St-Ignace, NB most people look at me and say, "you're kidding right?".

Then I usually laugh and say, no!!! I proceed by then telling them it is an Acadian village, and they are usually like, "what is that?".

Hi, my name is Mia Martina and I am an Acadian multi platinum singer/songwriter. If you only knew how much the ACADIAN word here is important to mention since I have travelled and performed across the world in my career, coming from a humble small town, I carry the resiliency of an Acadian. The Acadian culture is something that I'm so very proud to be part of and I wish Canadian's were a little bit more educated about how we came to be and the adversity we have faced. Knowing the commitment and strength of Acadian history has empowered me as a person and performer.

Let me give you a little bit of a history lesson.

In the 1630s, immigrants from Poitou and Anjou, France settled in Canada's maritime provinces. This is where the story of Acadians begins. These families, joined by families from several other European countries, created prosperous farming settlements around the Bay of Fundy. Over decades, the Acadians evolved a French-speaking North American culture distinct from the European cultures. Living in an area called La Cadie, they became known as Acadians. During this time, the French formed alliances with the two main Indigenous Peoples of the Acadia area, the Mi'kmaqs and the Maliseet. According to linguists, the word "Cadie" ("Lacadie" or "Acadie") may have derived from "Quoddy"—a word used by the Indigenous Peoples to designate a fertile area. It could also derive from the Mi' kmaq word "Algatig" meaning camp.

The area that became known as Acadia was inhabited for thousands of years by Indigenous Peoples, predominantly the Mi' kmaq.

In the 17th and 18th centuries, Britain and France vied for political control of Northeast, North America. Britain prevailed and required Acadians to sign an oath of allegiance to Britain. Acadians, whose economy was linked with French, English, and Indigenous Peoples communities, refused to sign or signed provisional oaths exempting them from taking up arms, thus becoming—to the British—a potential threat. Political tensions grew in the 18th century until Britain's culminating act to gain control of the region resulted in the Acadians' Great Upheaval. Beginning in 1755, Acadians became prisoners of war, and all who were captured were taken by ship and exiled in the British colonies along the eastern seaboard, or were sent by ship to England and France. Many died at sea. About 10,000 Acadians were uprooted—some say thousands more, with their businesses and farms burned behind them. Many fled into the interior of North America, aided by the Mi'kmaq.

In the decades following the upheaval, Acadians made their way back to what is now Québec and to Atlantic Canada, forming Acadian enclaves and communities which thrive today. One example is known as The Madawaska in northern ME and northern New Brunswick. In the 19th century, Acadians experienced a cultural renaissance which included the creation of French-language secondary schools and universities, as well as adopting the symbols of Acadia: the flag, patron saint, motto, and song.

Current French-language universities in Acadian Atlantic Canada include Université Sainte Anne, Church Point, NS (founded 1890), Université de Moncton, Moncton, NB (founded 1963), and newly formed Collège de l'Acadie.

In December 2003, the Canadian Federal Government agreed to issue a proclamation in the name of the Queen recognizing the wrongs the Acadians suffered during the exile. Beginning in 2005, on the 250th anniversary of the Great Upheaval, July 28th of every year was and will continue to be designated as "A Day of Commemoration of the Great Upheaval."

Today, Acadians world-wide continue to re-weave the fabric of their family history and heritage in the context of shared Acadian history and culture. Some Acadians are well known as writers, politicians, artists, musicians, and performers. Other Acadians are connecting with their identity through North American French, or through genealogy, beginning with their last name. Who are Acadians? They are one of North America's vibrant cultures maintaining their French language and culture in a bilingual setting.

I'm so happy to be a part of such a beautiful culture and to spread awareness since there are not many of us left and we always have to fight for our rights to be heard. My career accomplishments have helped me to aid other Acadian's find their voices and share with the world the education about our beautiful, resilient, and vibrant culture. I only hope to keep inspiring and growing so the future generations can keep our story alive.

I will leave you with this beautiful quote, *"To be Acadian is to have Pardon in your heart and to look forward with hope."* -Zachary Richard

References:

- https://www.thecanadianencyclopedia.ca/en/article/history-of-acadia
- https://www.cbc.ca/acadian/feature_acadian_origin.html
- https://umaine.edu/teachingcanada/culture-focus-acadia-acadians

MLLE ELIZABETH ANN

Swiss | German | French
www.mlleelizabethann.ca | ig: @mlle.elizabeth.ann
fb: @elizabeth.ann.author

Une femme anglophone
Écrit par Mlle Elizabeth Ann.

Imaginez que vous êtes une femme anglophone qui apprend le français au Canada.

Imaginez, également, que dans votre pays bilingue, vous ressentiez de la discrimination parce que vous parlez le français.

Imaginez que moi, une femme anglophone dans mon pays natal, je me sens telle une étrangère.

Je suis née au Canada mais je ne suis pas canadienne française. Dans notre pays, le français est couramment utilisé dans notre gouvernement, enseigné dans nos écoles, en fait c'est notre seconde langue. Il est rare par contre de l'entendre parler dans la plupart de nos provinces.

Pendant toute ma vie, je me suis intéressée à la langue française. J'étais la seule personne de ma famille qui désirait l'apprendre. Je me suis aussi intéressée à la culture, la musique, et la gastronomie française et ce, depuis mon plus jeune âge.

Malgré mon intérêt, je ne suis pas parfaite lorsque je communique. En effet, mon accent est un peu *bizarre* et je fais des erreurs de syntaxe ou de prononciation. Lors de mes efforts pour m'améliorer, tout le monde me répond en anglais et, tout de suite, je me sens dénigrée.

J'ai fait mes études universitaire en français et j'ai eu la chance de voyager dans plusieurs villes où l'on parle français. Mais pourquoi, alors, dans mon propre pays, est-ce que je me sens comme l'étrangère quand je parle notre deuxième langue?

C'est vrai qu'il existe une tension entre les anglophones et les francophones depuis des décennies. Je sais qu'il existe toujours des peuples qui se disputent ou ne sont pas d'accord, mais moi, une femme anglophone, je me suis engagée dans ma vie à enseigner cette belle langue et cette merveilleuse culture. J'ai le désir de partager cette passion afin que mes élèves puissent l'apprécier à sa juste valeur. Pourquoi, alors, cette frustration d'être répondu en anglais ou d'être moquée pour mon accent parce qu'il est différent.

Chaque jour au travail, j'entends des questions telles que : "Mlle, pourquoi dois-je apprendre le français? Pourquoi est-ce important?" J'entends également des commentaires tels que : "C'est stupide. Je n'aime pas le français. Je ne vais jamais l'utiliser après l'école secondaire." Mais malgré ces commentaires, je continue tout de même à partager ma passion et enseigner.

Je crois que c'est important de connaître, comprendre et apprécier les autres cultures, surtout celles qui sont célébrées partout dans ce beau pays qu'est le Canada. Étant Canadienne, je ne discrimine personne et je ne porte aucun préjudice envers ceux et celles qui tentent, tout comme moi, d'apprendre une langue différente. Et ce, surtout pour quelqu'un qui est né ici au Canada, un pays qui se dit bilingue et ouvert aux différences. Pourquoi, alors, certaines personnes me rabaisse lorsque je tente de m'exprimer librement dans une autre langue.

Imaginez qu'un jour, je me sente accueillie dans les autres provinces de mon pays sans jugement.

Imaginez également que mes étudiants ne souffrent pas de la même façon que moi.

Imaginez qu'on puisse s'accepter l'un l'autre pour la beauté que l'on possède en tant qu'être humain unique et diversifié. En plus, qu'on puisse se promettre mutuellement d'apprendre et de célébrer nos cultures pour mieux comprendre d'où on vient.

ENGLISH TRANSLATION

Imagine that you are an English-speaking woman who learns French in Canada.

Imagine equally that in your bilingual country, you experience discrimination for speaking French.

Imagine that I, an English-speaking woman in my native country, feel like a stranger.

I was born in Canada but I am not a French-Canadian. In our country French is commonly used in our government, taught in our schools, it is our second language—but it is uncommon to hear it spoken in most of our provinces.

During all my life, I was interested in the French language. I was the only person in my family who wanted to learn it. I have also been interested in French culture, music and gastronomy, from a very young age.

Despite my interest, I am not perfect when I communicate. In fact, my accent is a bit *weird* and I make mistakes with sentence structure or pronunciation. During my efforts to improve myself, everyone answers me in English and right away I feel belittled.

I completed my post secondary studies in French and I've had the chance to travel to several cities where French is spoken. But why in my own country do I feel like a foreigner when I speak our second language?

It is true that there has been a history of tension between Anglophones and Francophones for decades. I know there are still people (populations) who fight or disagree but I, an English-speaking woman, have committed my life to teaching this beautiful language, this wonderful culture. I want to share this passion so that my students can fully appreciate it. Why, then, this frustration at being answered in English or being laughed at for my accent because it is different.

Every day at work I hear questions like, "Miss, why do I have to learn French? Why is it important?" Or I hear comments like, "It's stupid. I do not like French. I'm never going to use French after high school." But despite these comments, I still continue to share my passion and to teach.

I believe it is important to know, understand and appreciate other cultures, especially those that are celebrated all over this beautiful country of Canada. Being Canadian, I do not discriminate against anyone and I do not hold prejudice to those who try, like me, to learn a different language. This is especially true for someone who was born here in Canada, a country that claims to be bilingual and open to differences. Why, then, some people demean me when I try to express myself freely in another language?

Imagine that one day, I feel welcomed in the other provinces of my country.

Also imagine that my students do not suffer the same way as I do.

Imagine that we can accept each other for the beauty that we possess as unique and diverse human beings, and allow each other to learn and celebrate what we can share with each other.

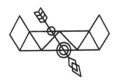

Chapter Two

GIRL WHOSE SOUL SHINES THROUGH HER SMILE

"Today is a good day to start walking away from anyone or anything that causes you more angst than joy."

CHARLEYNE OULTON

Charleyne Oulton

Scottish | Prussian

www.coachcharleybrown.com

ig: @coach.charley.brown | fb: @coachcharleybrown
goodreads: charleyne oulton

Portraiture by: Katie Jean Photography, Mill Bay BC

Charleyne Oulton, Coach Charley Brown, is a confident, happy, mom of three children who lives on beautiful Vancouver Island, BC. She is genuine, experienced, and passionate about creating and maintaining a life full of peace and joy. She is a well appreciated Health and Wellness Coach, contributing award winning author in books: *On Her Plate*; *Dear Time, Are You On My Side; Her Art of Surrender* and *Her Art of Surrender e2*; *You've Got This Mama, Too*; and is writing in upcoming books: *Mama's Gotta Work*; *Being Mama*; and *She's No Longer Silent*. Charleyne is also a reserve member of the Royal Canadian Navy, even through the busy and beautiful chaos of raising a family. It is her purpose to inspire women, and specifically the busy, overworked, and exhausted mothers around the world, to remember their personal strength and rediscover their worth and joy. That they, along with us all, are deserving of living a life filled with health, happiness, and harmony in our beautiful country.

Everything comes to you at the right moment. Be patient. Be grateful. Believe in destiny and fate. Have faith that, what is meant to be will be. The easiest way to create and live a fulfilled and happy life is to master *going with the flow,* and to do what is right for *you* right *now*. But I also know how hard these practices can be. Change can feel terrifying, and so can divorce. Being courageous for yourself is not always the easiest choice. Doing what is right for you can sometimes feel impossible and unattainable. Your ultimate happiness is worth fighting for, and so is your joy. Joy is HOPE, which always lies within you.

> *Today is a good day to start walking away*
> *from anyone or anything that causes you more*
> *angst than joy.*

Divorc, Divorci, Divorce, Divorzio, Divorcio . . . No matter the language, I do not like this word. I think it's ugly, and it makes me feel bad about myself. I never envisioned myself as a divorced mother of three. Even though my marriage was toxic for my soul and often left me feeling both drained and depleted, I would not have wished divorce for us, or for our children. Yet, here I am separated awaiting divorce.

Through my divorce, I have learned that sometimes in life we must allow change to happen, surrender our expectations, and accept our current situation. I was stuck in a day-to-day routine that was not fulfilling my needs or fully meeting my deepest desires—lying to myself every single day. I had settled and accepted my role as a wife and mother, and nothing more. I'd taught myself to see the good and appreciate *only* those moments. The truth was that I was not happy, and those who knew me knew it. Even though I put on the apron, the lipstick, the smile, and the appearance of a happily married housewife, my soul craved more. Knowing I was capable of living a different life, but refusing to listen to my intuition, or admit this out loud out of fear. *This was what all wives go through, right? This is what marriage feels like, right? Isn't it supposed to be hard, and isn't this "hard" what is best for our children?* These are some of the lies I convinced myself to believe.

I want to give you the purest, most sincere and genuine advice I have been given: always, always, always listen to your gut and follow your heart. Those goosebumps and chills you sometimes feel, that little voice inside your head, and those whispers and nudges from your soul are all trying to tell you something. Pay attention. I used to fear divorce, being alone, dating, and the judgement of what my family and society would think of my failed marriage. I used to ignore all the warning signs, and *red flags*. This was the life I thought I wanted? To me, the D word was the ultimate failure. Even though I was married to the wrong person, I had accepted the role as a wife and I tried very hard to fully find true happiness. The problem was, I was looking in the wrong place. Happiness and joy come from within. I deserve to be a priority in my life. Once I remembered this, I was no longer as fearful of the change that was ultimately happening.

It is an incredible experience to be stripped of everything I once thought defined me. My title, role, possessions, career, family, vehicles, and bank accounts. My entire world was shifting right in front of me and so much of it was out of my control. I learned very quickly that I must become a master at maintaining balance, managing stress, and simplifying my life. My house, belongings, time with my children, assets, debts, were all being divided. It was an earth shattering chapter of life.

We all need something different from life and have our own path to walk. Sometimes we need to do what scares us the most. We may need to make some tough choices and choose the road less travelled. Sometimes you need to follow your intuition and even go against your family or religious beliefs. I encourage you to keep an open heart, remain positive, and trust life's journey. Stop being a worrier and start being a warrior! It was my impending divorce, which brought me to applying for the Royal Canadian Navy.

I had to start over. Begin again. And I was terrified.

I knew I wanted a career that made a difference, came with benefits, pension, and to prove to my children that starting over can be full of adventure and fun. So with all the courage I could muster, I sent off an email to a recruiter and nine months later I was being sworn in as a Reserve

Member of the Canadian Armed Forces (CAF) with my family proudly watching.

Spontaneity makes for the very best memories and adventures. I was given only twenty hours notice, ten months after joining the Navy, that I would be leaving for fourteen days to participate as a paddler in the Royal Canadian Navy's (RCN) Canoe and assist as ground support in the Pulling Together Canoe Journey 2019 #PCTJ2019. Being a member of the CAF, I am half packed ready to go, always, but still was finding myself full of doubt and anxiety as my fiancé sat with me as I quickly packed my rucksack, and together we went over the childrens' schedules, and upcoming to-do lists. I was taking a giant step out of my comfort zone, about to do something I wouldn't have thought possible a year ago. Sometimes you just need to go off the grid and get your soul right. As a mother to three children who at the time were aged fifteen, thirteen, and twelve, this was a rare gift. So as nervous as I was, I kissed my family goodbye and focused on the task at hand, with hopes of carving out a few moments to relax.

Since 2007 the RCN has been providing safety boats, navigation, advice, and scheduling support to PCTJ. After twelve years of ground and safety support, the RCN was, for the first time, sending two crews to participate; one for ground and safety, and one crew to fully immerse and participate in the journey by paddling in the RCN's brand new canoe. Thus deepening our relationships and cultural understanding with First Nations communities.

Vulnerability is the birthplace of love,
belonging, joy, courage, empathy and creativity.
It is the source of hope, accountability and
authenticity. If we want greater clarity in
our purpose or deeper and more meaningful
spiritual lives, vulnerability is the path.

These are the thoughts that were circling through my head as I openly embraced and connected with others during the 2019 Pulling Together Canoe Journey #PCTJ2019 in the beautiful communities of Powell River, British Columbia and Tla'amin Nation as a member of the RCN.

Although I grew up in Canada, and Canada is a diverse country, this was my first time experiencing all aspects of the Coast Salish people up close and personal. I try to be open and inclusive in my relationships with fellow human beings, but this was a new opportunity for me to learn first hand about First Nation culture. I realize that being born in Canada means that I have experienced diversity my whole entire life. Fortunately, I have experienced many cultures and I have been raised to be open and accountable. Unfortunately, prior to participating in #PCTJ2019, I had only seen a Pacific Northwest Canoe in the museum, and now I was going to be paddling in one! How incredible to be welcomed and fully involved in the protocols, ceremonies, and experience of a Canoe Journey.

"The canoe is the single most important physical manifestation of Northwest Coast First Nations' culture. They go back to the Great Flood myth, and exist at the nexus between technology and living beings. Blessed at each step of their transformation and hardened by the forces of fire and water, these canoes came to represent whole clans and communities. In canoe journeys, the canoe almost leads its crew along, its own journey of ten thousand years or more an exemplar of unity and power, of daunting persistence, and spiritual transport. The canoe's technology is older than time, but still perfectly fitting for people seeking to explore and know the ocean. The Northwest Coast canoe provides the maximum amount of boat for the minimum amount of material, and represents unity and teamwork, as well as strength training and health. The canoe served many purposes such as traveling, hunting, mobility and warring with other tribes."[1]

As soon as we arrived at the Tla'amin Nation we were welcomed with warm greetings and proceeded to set up our issued Mod Tents that would be our home for the duration of our trip. Members of the community had opened up their homes, so that we could do laundry and shower. All our meals were cooked in the community hall and this is where we were able to really bond and befriend one another. I was introduced to and gifted a Devil's Club Bracelet, which I will forever cherish from a young lad named Finn. I was taught by Ed Hill, a Gibsons Paddle Club member, that "these bracelets are made of leather and have four beads, red, black, yellow, and white, and a small cylindrical piece of cream coloured wood—Devil's Club. The four beads represent the four directions, and

---

1   Neel, 1., Stewart, 1., & Suttles, 1. (2010). "Northwest Coast Canoes." Published by The Bill Reid Centre – Simon Fraser University. Burnaby, BC, Canada.

also, they represent the four races of the world—all people. The wood is a very old, culturally significant plant for the native people for medicine, for protection, and even as a weapon." The gifting of this is an ancient tradition and is gifted to someone with good intentions to help protect the receiver from any bad spirits on the water while on a canoe journey. "They travel with the paddlers on their journey, and as they are given away, they create a weave of wonderful friendship around the world. Isn't it significant that an ancient native tradition can have so much power, so much magic attached to it, even in our modern day world?"

For the first time in my life I witnessed a culturally rich display of drumming, singing, dancing and prayers in a Waking Up Ceremony for a canoe. I was fortunate enough to participate in the Waking Up Ceremony for the RCNs new canoe with cedar. Cedar is used for clan poles, masks, canoes, paddles, carvings, and for brushings. I was taught by an elder that cedar represents the root of all life. Watching the elders wake up our canoe by cleaning it with the beautiful cedar branches was absolutely breathtaking. During the ceremony, our canoe and ourselves were brushed with cedar and I was given the spirit name "Girl Whose Soul Shines Through Her Smile," as tears shed slowly from my eyes.

Mother Earth we sing to you. In absolute love and gratitude.

I learned that music plays an integral role in the life of Indigenous peoples. They sing in ceremonial purposes, for recreation, expression, and even for healing. It was an honor to be allowed to learn and sing some of their songs such as: *The Water Song, The Challenge Song, The Competition Song, The Co-Ed Song,* and *The Unity Song.* A few times throughout our journey we tied all of our canoes together and stories were shared and songs were sung. It was so powerful and beautiful and every time we sang together I felt such a flow of energy, a presence like static electricity that was flowing through my veins with every verse sung. It was such a good way for us to join as one, release endorphins naturally, and cope with the physical and mental stresses of pulling. When pulling for days on end, it is so important to remain present and live in the now. Not to get lost in worry about where you are going, or how long until you arrive there, not to think negatively about the waves and currents, but rather accept all of the chaos around you. The weather, your canoe family, and the ocean conditions are ever changing, but singing helped ground and unite us. It was amazing to witness others return to a baseline state of calm quickly with each song.

I love people who are so compassionate and humane, who spread kind words everywhere they go and help anyone in need, even when they are strangers. People who choose to be soft, delicate and welcoming. I learned the value of community and togetherness from the ancient wisdom from the native people I was lucky enough to spend time with. It is absolutely ironic and disappointing to me that I grew up on Vancouver Island, in British Columbia which is home to Kwakwaka'wakw, Coast Salish, and Nuu-chah-nulth communities, and yet I had never, ever stepped foot on Native Territory once in my life. I am eternally grateful to have participated in Pulling Together Journey 2019, and for the people who opened up their homes, nation, and shared their traditions with me.

After spending time on their land and with their people I learned that I AM a capable, beautiful, and intelligent woman. I was reminded to forgive myself for all the times I was naive, for all the times I should have been hard when I was soft. I learned how to be kind to myself and to Mother Earth. I will never forget the lessons and significance of Sage, Cedar, and Eagles.

Remember friends, the most beautiful people we have known are those who have known defeat, suffering, struggle, and loss, and have found their way out of those depths and continue to challenge themselves and push past every limit. I now have a greater appreciation for generational wisdom and have learned to truly respect the very soil we live on. I learned to let go of my embarrassment and shame I felt with the title of divorcee, and rather focus on the growth that came with that lesson and experience.

KARLA SMITH

Barbadian (Bajan) | English
www.kslifecoach.com

This is not new to me.

I was born into a racist culture and have lived with oppression, bias, racism, inequality, and stereotypes all my life. I have a lifetime of stories to share. Situations, comments, and instances, some subtle, some not so subtle, that I have pushed down in order to cope and live productively.

This is not new to me.

In moments of injustice to others that make it onto the news cycle, my experiences seep out, enveloping me with the reminder that this is always part of my experience.

This is not new to me.

My kids, my family, and my friends of colour are forced to navigate the ever-present bias that we are not equal. Our outrage is not over the current incident in your consciousness. Our outrage exists because we all have a lifetime of incidents and we keep wondering when you will notice.

This is not new to me.

As a young girl, nearly forty years ago, my sister and I were holding hands with our white dad walking down Rue St Denis in Montreal, when a man stepped up to us, spat at my dad's feet and called him a "sick old bastard." His assumption was that we were teenage escorts instead of children of a white man.

This is not new to me.

In grade 11 a boy I was dating invited me to a semi-formal party at his parents' club. I remember dressing up and taking the bus to his house at Lawrence and Avenue Rd. As I stood in the front entrance of his house, his parents came down the stairs to meet me, his mom stopped, gasped and told him I couldn't go with them to their club. I wasn't welcome simply because of my skin colour.

This is not new to me.

A few years ago, in a small-town drugstore, security followed me around, aisle by aisle as I did my shopping, lurking just far enough away that I could not ask him what he was doing. I regret not going up to him to ask why he was following me. Years of conditioning has taught me not to be disruptive or confrontational.

This is not new to me.

Last year (2019) at an upscale store in Yorkdale Mall, Toronto, my son and I went in to buy him a coat and could not get service from any of the salespeople. When we returned with my white husband, they immediately came over to serve him. Seeing this through my son's eyes is always heartbreaking. We won't shop there again.

These are the easier stories to share because they are blatant. I know that you know they are offensive. I trust they will be acknowledged as racist and "bad."

What is much more difficult and insidious are the comments and actions that feel harmless to others. The things people question as racist or think I'm too sensitive about.

The extra long stare when my family walks into a small-town McDonald's.

People ask if they can touch my hair because it looks so soft and puffy.

People insisting how lucky I am because I don't ever have to get a tan.

People asking me "Do you work here?"

A racist joke told in a group that everyone laughs at even if it feels wrong.

Being "randomly" searched at the airport so many more times than my white husband.

Watching people cross the street when they see my boys coming.

This is not new to me.

I pray that as I write this we are at the beginning of a new collective awareness. I am hopeful that my experiences will somehow help to crack open the silence, apathy, ignorance, and lack of knowledge that has been going on for far too long. I believe transformation is possible when we lean in, learn, listen, share, and act. Together we have the opportunity to create powerful change. I'm ready for something new, are you?

Chapter Three

FROM FAKIN' THE BACON TO MAKIN' THE BACON

"When you think about it, most failures aren't really failures— they're valuable, teachable moments in our lives."

KAREN SWYSZCZ

Karen Swyszcz

Filipino | Chinese | Spanish

www.makinthebacon.com

ig: @makinthebacon1 | fb: @makinthebacon1
t: @makinthebacon1

Karen Swyszcz is naturally an introvert, but given the right type of situation, she can become extroverted. Growing up, Karen had a creative streak in her, but was led to believe that following a traditional career path would bring her great happiness and success. Throughout her twenties and early thirties, she tried to find a suitable job, but often found herself bored and frustrated. *Makinthebacon* began as a passion project to escape the monotony of her government job. Little did she know that this hobby blog would lead to a drastic career change and the start of her own consulting business, from 2017-2020.

Prior to starting her own consulting business, she worked as an analyst at an ad tech startup. Accepting this job was a huge risk, but it was the best decision she has ever made.

Karen has a Bachelor of Science degree in biochemistry from the University of Waterloo. Karen is a faculty member of Continuing and Professional Studies at Sheridan College where she teaches the Blogging For Fun & Profit and Effective Strategies For Social Media courses. She is a certified BodyPump and BodyAttack instructor. She loves the group fitness atmosphere and enjoys teaching these classes several times a week.

Karen has the natural ability to seek and create opportunities. She is passionate about helping others tell their story and believes your passions can also help you make the bacon.

We often associate certain foods with certain memories. For a brief period in my life, I couldn't order takeout Chinese food from my favourite Chinese Restaurant. Here's why.

There were two significant moments where I had reached my breaking point with my government job. I can't remember in what order they were, but one was when I exploded in an onslaught of f-bombs in front of my boss, his supervisor, and whoever happened to be in the lunchroom. The other time was while I was ordering takeout Chinese food. I had a long day and hadn't eaten since lunchtime, but the restaurant was getting ready to close. I still remember that evening, crying and begging for food as the owners told me they were closing and I wouldn't be served. I was well aware of how extreme my reaction was, but I didn't care. They eventually gave in. Right then and there I knew it wasn't just the feeling of hunger, but also the feeling of complete exhaustion and defeat. My government job was sucking the life out of me.

This is my story—the over-achiever who experiences failure as an adult. Over and over and over again. I went back to the drawing board more times than I can count, starting from scratch every single time. Stumbling, crawling through the process in an attempt to find out what it was I was actually supposed to be doing with my life.

Growing up, I was led to believe that the path to becoming a successful adult was this: go to school, work hard, get good grades, get a job, get married, buy a house, and have kids. Yet to me, it all seemed robotic. While I ended up ticking off most of those boxes, I felt there was much more to life.

When I was young, failure was not an option. It was never presented as an option. It was never really discussed. All I remember was my mom wanted A's, whereas my dad was more laid back and said it was fine as long as I passed. Throughout childhood, I excelled and had a desire to continuously excel. I am the eldest daughter of Filipino immigrants. My parents had moved to Canada on separate occasions in the 1970s, in search of a better life and better job opportunities. Within many Asian cultures and some European cultures, there is always pressure to do well: to go to school and eventually become a doctor, lawyer, accountant, etc.—a white collar job that your parents could brag about to their friends and family here in Canada and back home. I wanted to make my parents proud and be proud of myself. I didn't want to be the outsider, even though deep down, I knew I was a rebel and was meant to embark on a journey that would lead to a meaningful career to me—not to others.

When I was growing up, there were very few children of minority backgrounds in my neighbourhood and in my elementary school. More often than not, I was either one of the two non-Caucasian children and the only student of Asian descent.

While being considered the smartest in class was an achievement for parents and teachers (and because it made my parents proud), at the same time, it was also a burden. In addition to being teased for getting good grades, I was constantly teased by others for having a Chinese last name: Yap. One can only imagine the words that rhyme with it: slap, flap, crap, etc. Kids would often tell me to stop "yapping" so much. This was ironic because I was one of the quiet kids. While this was happening, I silently declared to myself that I would marry someone with a generic last name such as Smith or Anderson, so I wouldn't be made fun of anymore. Interestingly enough, I ended up marrying someone with not only a hard to spell last name, but a last name that is also hard to pronounce. Read this: no vowels.

Some people assumed I was Chinese based on my last name, while others saw some sort of other Asian, but not necessarily Filipino. Depending on who you talked to, I was considered to be more fair (there is also Spanish heritage from my mom's side) and not as brown.

The constant teasing of my last name made me feel ashamed of my heritage. In addition to wishing for a different last name, I often wished my hair and my eyes were a different colour. Since I couldn't change my physical appearance at the time, I tried my best to be Canadian through things such as the food. I brought sandwiches to school like the other students and made sure my mom didn't cook anything that smelled or tasted "weird" whenever I had friends over.

My parents were also quite overprotective. I wasn't allowed to do many of the things my Canadian friends could do such as going to sleepovers. I even had a chaperone (an older cousin) accompany me when I first attended birthday parties! It took a lot of convincing, but eventually I was able to attend these occasions on my own.

I was enrolled in extracurricular activities such as piano, ballet, and math enrichment (basically extra math homework to help me get ahead). My cousins were also enrolled in piano and math enrichment, so I assumed that was the reason why my parents did the same for me. I knew that they loved me very much and only wanted the best for me. Looking back on it, I wish my parents had enrolled me in the activities that my friends were doing such as Girl Guides, summer day camp, and soccer lessons.

By high school, I knew that I needed to go away for university. I was starving for freedom and independence. In my mind, I felt that if I was given that opportunity, I could prove to my parents that I could be successful on my own.

It was the complete opposite of what I had expected.

I experienced failure or what felt like it for the first time during my first semester of university. I was having trouble adjusting to living away from home, not getting along with my roommate, struggling to make friends, and the workload felt like the equivalent of a full-time job. I didn't know how to manage my time. I didn't know how to manage any of it. Without an ability to cope with failure and loneliness, I became very depressed and had to seek counselling, ultimately flunking my first semester entirely. For the longest time, I was so ashamed of everything that had happened during that first semester. I had barely entered adulthood and already I felt like I was a complete failure.

Not even really sure what I wanted to do after that, I decided to pursue a degree in the sciences. Although I knew deep down inside this was not my desired path, I finished the degree—to please my parents. In hindsight, I should have taken a year off or dropped out of school to figure out what I wanted to do with my life. For almost ten years, this cycle continued. I was trying desperately to figure out how to be satisfied with my job, and how to make something out of my life. From project management to personal training, nothing seemed like it was a good fit. With each job I became restless, bored, and frustrated very quickly. My career path resembled more of a jungle gym or rock-climbing wall versus climbing the corporate ladder. Even though it was like comparing apples to oranges, I looked at everyone around me. All of them seemed to be on this upward trajectory and here I was constantly asking myself why things weren't turning out that way for me.

Why couldn't I get my life together?

Growing up I had a creative side. I had enjoyed doodling, writing, drawing out different styles of the alphabet—all the things that were artistic. There was no encouragement from my parents to pursue any of these things at a serious level though. It was only meant to be a hobby.

In their eyes, these were not considered successful endeavors and therefore, were never presented to me as feasible options to pursue in life.

I'll never forget a conversation I had with one of my high school English teachers. She was asking if I was planning to study English or journalism in university. Much to her surprise, I replied that I had applied for engineering programs. She very likely saw the writing on the wall, when I was too blinded by my mission to succeed at making everyone else proud.

After having quit numerous jobs with no backup plan, I eventually landed a position with the government in the food inspection sector. At the time, it seemed like a no-brainer because I was only working part-time and needed the additional income. Getting accepted into the government in my late twenties meant I would work there for twenty-five to thirty years and receive a healthy pension upon retirement. *Success!*

It's important to note this wasn't a typical cushy office job or one where I frequented restaurants for inspection. It was a job where I worked with bacon, or to be more accurate, inspected bacon before it became the bacon you eat. I worked at a slaughterhouse. With a 6:30 a.m. start and being covered in blood and guts on a daily basis, it was unlike any other job I had before. This was a whole new level of misalignment for me. I knew meat was expensive, but to see a significant part of the process that made it so expensive was very eye-opening.

For the first few years, I was proud that I inspected food prior to it being used for consumption both locally and internationally. However, it wasn't without comments or looks of disgust or horror from others that only seemed to grow in number with time. I began to feel moments of shame and embarrassment for my own career. I couldn't shake them off. Here I was, playing a crucial role in keeping food safe for Canadians, only to have people look down on what I did. From then on, when I was asked what I did for a living, I gave a very vague description and quickly changed the subject. I then began to see myself as a complete failure all over again.

I graduated with a biochemistry degree from a prestigious university and worked at this job for almost five years, but despite my best efforts I had seen no career progression. There was a career aptitude test you were required to take in order to qualify for new or advanced positions. I failed it every single time. It almost seemed as if no matter how many times I took it, I couldn't change my way of thinking. I couldn't hide the fact that I wasn't internally aligned with the line of work I had pursued. *What was I to do?* The sense of obligation to stay was overwhelming. Feeling trapped with the responsibility of a mortgage, and growing increasingly doubtful that I would be able to find success at yet another new gig; I felt incredibly lost and unhappy.

I thought that if I went away on vacation, the unhappiness would disappear. It was nothing but a temporary fix. The misery quickly reappeared when I returned to my job. I wasn't planning on getting married and having a wedding, but I thought that it would be a nice distraction from my job. Planning for the wedding only created more unhappiness and stress for me, especially financial. It wasn't even a big, extravagant wedding, (I purchased my engagement ring and wedding rings online and kept the wedding party small), but we all know how wedding costs can creep up on you.

One day while I was researching ways to make more money (to help pay for the wedding), I came across blogging. I decided to start a blog in hopes of softening the blow of wedding expenses. *It ended up serving a much greater purpose.* The blog was a place where I could share my thoughts and experiences anonymously with the world. I had lost touch with creative writing when I began university and blogging helped rekindle the long-lost love for expressing myself through the written word. Personality wise, I am an introvert and experience social anxiety to a certain extent. Hence, I always felt I was better at expressing myself through writing versus speaking. I turned to blogging as a way to connect with others who shared the same experiences I had or were in the process of going through it. Not only that, it was a place where I could express my passion for personal finance, hence the name, *Makinthebacon*. Since I was so focused on trying to build a career, the blog often got put on the back burner.

I threw myself into the career-advancing process by joining the health and safety committee and spearheading a project on career development within my government agency. I had countless meetings and phone calls with upper management to discuss transferring to a different department or better job opportunities within my own department. Even though I was putting in a great deal of effort to create opportunities for myself, I was going nowhere. It was as if my department felt it was easiest to have me stay put in my current position, and that career progression was not necessary. For an ambitious over-achiever like myself, this felt like career suicide. Feeling universally blocked from every angle in my traditional career, I decided to make a sharp u-turn and re-direct my efforts into the personal project I previously had not made any time for: the blog. At that point, I knew that for me, *anything* was better than staying stagnant at a job with no promising future for the next twenty-five to thirty years. From then on, every coffee break, lunch break, and spare moment I had on the weekend was spent working on the blog.

That was when opportunities started to appear through the blog. I was still working at the slaughterhouse, but I began to toy with the idea of a drastic career change. I didn't feel I was at a point where I wanted to work for myself. All I knew was that deep down I needed to leave the government agency entirely. I took inventory of the skills I had learned alongside starting a blog and began applying to jobs with startups. From marketing to sales to operations, I applied to every job that I thought I could figure out while still working. I didn't have any experience working at a startup or formal education in business or technology, but I had grit, initiative, a willingness to learn: fail fast, and try again.

Yes, fail—I had become an expert at it by this point. It was a skill!

All I needed was for someone to give me a chance, and when the opportunity arose to join a startup, I knew it was now or never and I had to go for it. *It was my Hail Mary.*

I remember crying to my fiancé (now husband) on the phone when I told him. For the first time, in a very long time, I was crying not out of sadness and frustration, but out of happiness.

When I announced my departure from my job, I was met with a lot of doubt and criticism from my family and coworkers. Many of them were shocked by my decision and told me that I was making a huge mistake. Leaving a stable job with all the benefits, pension, and paid time off (plus taking a significant pay cut) was a scary and risky move, but it was one of the best decisions I have ever made. I learned so much while working at the start-up—more than I had ever learned during the four and a half years at my government job. I do not regret it at all because it was such a great experience, even though the opportunity was short lived. I was let go from the startup company in 2017. *Another fail!*

Or was it? Although I had been taking steps to transition the blog and use it more as a platform to showcase my consulting services, I had only scratched the surface. Yet in the perils of my termination, instead of looking for another nine-to-five job, I decided to listen to my gut again and trust that I was meant to be on a different path. I took another societally deemed risk and decided to focus all of my efforts on building my blog consulting business full-time. I told everyone that I created content by blogging about my experiences, lessons, and learnings, and would teach others how to do the same.

Once again, I was faced with doubt and criticism from the people who were closest to me. It was getting a little easier to take by this point. Even though I wasn't entirely ready (if there ever is such a feeling), I knew I had to call again on my superpowers: the willingness to work hard when things got tough, fail fast, and try again. I would fight like hell every day to work on the consulting business and prove the naysayers wrong.

I'll be honest. There are times when I think how much easier it could have been if I had been doing blog consulting full-time with another company or if I already had a successful side-business and had reached a point where I could make the leap. I couldn't help but feel jealous of these people who appeared to make these seamless transitions while I was busy failing my way forward. I found solace in the hard fact that I had been playing it safe for the majority of my life, doing what everyone else was doing and it didn't really get me anywhere. Something absolutely needed to change!

Eckhart Tolle said, *"Any action is often better than no action, especially if you have been stuck in an unhappy situation for a long time. If it is a mistake, at least you learn something, in which case it's no longer a mistake. If you remain stuck, you learn nothing."*

These days I do a lot more risk-taking and find myself looking forward to failing at new things that I try in my business. The difference now is that I see it as a sign of trying, learning, and gaining experience from it. I also listen to my gut more, as it was only when I began to listen to it that things started falling into place. *Who knew?* It's funny how things end up happening or how pieces start falling into place. Looking back at everything that has happened so far in my life, I feel as if I have come full circle. I used to be very embarrassed and ashamed of my story because I didn't represent the traditional idea of success: stable job, big house, nice car, and a couple of kids. Then I finally realized that the idea of success is whatever you want it to be. It wasn't until just a few years ago that I realized how important it was for me to tell my story because other people might be feeling the same way.

As unorthodox as it may be, starting a blog changed my life. It gave me desirable skills and unique job opportunities such as teaching continuing education courses at a world-renowned college on blogging and social media. It enabled me to start a consulting business and become a contributing author for not only this book, but also for the best-selling book in women's health, *Fitness To Freedom*. The blog gave me the courage to take more risks, try new things, and believe that anything is possible. My most recent endeavors include launching a business & technology podcast, and co-founding a social enterprise to connect Filipino-Canadian entrepreneurs and professionals throughout Canada and beyond. I believe that the latter came from my experiences as a child, the need to connect more with my heritage and the desire to see more representation at conferences, in certain industries, and in high-profile positions.

To all the women out there who feel stuck in life or in their careers, I want to tell you that it's normal and ok to feel stuck, but it's not ok to remain stuck and not do anything about it. We have a choice. We *always* have a choice.

Chapter Four

BE YOUR OWN NORTH STAR

*"One star at a time, light up
the dark."*

SHIRIN ARIFF

Shirin Ariff

Indian | Bengali

www.shirinariff.com

ig: @shirinariff | fb: @shirinariff | li: Shirin Ariff
t: @shirinariff | Goodreads: Shirin Ariff

Shirin is an inspirational speaker, an award-winning author, and a women's empowerment coach, committed to helping immigrant women find their own strength. Shirin curates Spoken Lives (Toronto West), a monthly event where four women share their story with an audience of both men and women, to touch, move, and inspire them. Shirin is also a Founding Member of Immigrant Women in Business (an organisation for women entrepreneurs) and represents India.

After braving immigration to Canada and surviving Thyroid Cancer, Shirin understands adversity. Despite the lemons that life handed her, she dug deep and found resilience. Today, Shirin can relate to women who are feeling defeated. She empowers women through her Be Your Own North Star Program to become their own guiding force.

No matter what struggle we are facing, we have the power within ourselves to overcome it. Her Shining Star Movement fosters a culture of resilience, independence, self-expression, and freedom.

It was 2003 and I was teaching world geography to middle school students in India. We learned about Canada being the land of snow and the magical Northern Lights. The idea of living in a log cabin fascinated me. I had seen pictures of them in the many storybooks I had read. I thought I knew everything about lumbering in Canada; there were two whole chapters on that! We read about the Canadian Rockies, the Prairies, and the Great Canadian Shield. Little did I know that I would live so close to Lake Ontario and walk along its shores later in life!

While my students were busy taking a quiz on Canada or working on a given class assignment, I would often catch myself drifting away in my thoughts. You see, I was newly-married. My new husband lived in Canada. I was going to join him soon to start our newly married life together and I was waiting eagerly for my spousal visa to arrive. We had just got married in India a few months prior and he had left soon after our honeymoon. It was so hard to live apart.

I dreamed of my new life in Canada. Would I be teaching about India to Canadian students like the way I teach about Canada to my students in India? I wondered. What would my Canadian home look like? Would it have a slanting roof and a backyard with cherry trees? Would we have to dress like Eskimos? I could have a giant real

Christmas tree and not the fake plastic ones that I decorated in India for the holidays. There was also a Loreto Abbey in Toronto! I was a Loreto girl. I am sure the Loreto Sisters would love me and give me a chance to teach in their Canadian school.

Sabah, my daughter from my first marriage, was immigrating with me. Her life would be so good! Of course she would go to a Loreto School in Canada as well.

We had been playing basketball in India. I had not taken a beginner's French course at Alliance Francaise for nothing. I had even learned to cook the not-so-Indian dishes like roast beef and stew. Oh and Celine Dion and Bryan Adams—they were my favourite Canadian singers! I loved their songs already. This would be my very first experience of being in the western world—the glamorous, the progressive, the prosperous land of sweetness, where mother earth pours out her sweet love—the land of the Maple tree.

The past four years since my first marriage ended in a divorce in India, it had been very stressful and miserable. We were homeless and shunting between relatives' homes in different cities as my first marriage to a drug addict had failed. We had no money of our own until I began teaching. Sabah and I slept on floors and lived out of plastic grocery bags. I was degraded and humiliated for being a divorced woman with a child. We were encumbrances. I cooked, cleaned, and did chores in relatives' homes in lieu of having a place to stay.

My new husband, my second marriage, had stood by me for the seemingly long time it took to get my spousal visa. My day of departure had arrived. On October 28, I boarded a plane with my daughter Sabah, to come home to Canada. We were relieved that we had severed ties with anything or anyone that diminished us for being women.

We landed in Toronto after flying for twenty-two hours. Finally we would be home, in our *own* home. Canada was our promise of the love and the family that we were so hungry for, and a future we couldn't wait to live.

The first jolt came in the discovery that the promised house on the lake was actually a room in Parkdale, Toronto: a working-class neighbourhood, with a large percentage of low-income households. My new husband dropped us home from the airport. He said he would be back the next morning and left us alone within a few minutes of arriving at the apartment. My blood ran cold as I looked at my young daughter. This was the beginning of my life in Canada. What followed next were eight years of torture. I endured endless emotional and verbal abuse. I thought I had left behind all the verbal violence, malicious gossip, and dowry taunting back home in India. I had married a Canadian and was in the land of freedom. But I was wrong. Even though I lived in Canada, I did not enjoy or even quite understand what was different about being Canadian. What different values would I need to embrace? My home continued to breed negativity and disempowerment for me. I had no respect and self-worth. I was reduced to a slave woman in my own home.

The first few years, I had no friends. My life was mundane. I had to fulfill various responsibilities in my husband's office. I was his secretary, office administrator, property manager, and janitor. At home I was his chef, laundry woman, and wife. My life was strenuous not only because that's how immigrants live in Canada, but for several reasons. I was often reminded that I did not bring any dowry with me and not to forget that I was not a virgin, but a divorced woman with a child before I married him.

A few years into the marriage, I had a paralysis that distorted my face and now I was ugly. My life got worse. In India, at least I was earning some money for the work I did as a teacher. In Canada, my husband never paid me for my sweat and skills. Just the way the dynamics were in India back then, my husband in Canada, kept control of the money that I worked for and called it *ours*. Once in a while he threw some change at me. I felt like a beggar and didn't dare to ask for more.

A good wife never asks questions. Silence is her most sought after virtue. She signs all papers without reading them. She is not demanding of her husband's time and money. She earns a place in heaven when she endures. She is loyal and trusts her man, no matter how he treats her. I was playing that game with him full on because I wanted his love, his acknowledgement, and appreciation, and as a bonus, *that* heaven I was promised. My present life was so tumultuous and insecure, but my after-life was paradise guaranteed.

That trance dancing to his tunes came to an end. The spell was broken. By 2013, I had three children from him and a cancer that had spread to my lymph nodes. I was afraid that I was going to die. As I lay on the surgery table in the operating room, I made a promise to myself, that if I lived, I would save myself and my children from this miserable life of abuse. I was done with playing a victim of drama, jealousy, control, isolation, brainwashing, gaslighting, sabotage, blame, destructive criticism, and targeting. We deserved better. That moment adversity gave me a gift. And in that moment, I found my True North. I was freed.

From then on, I took charge of my life and for the first time in nine whole years of being in Canada, I began to explore what being a Canadian woman really meant. What support did I have as a citizen? What rights did I have? What possibilities could I create for myself and my children in this country of abundance? How could I lift myself up and leave an empowering legacy for my children?

My first progressive action was to choose being happily divorced over being miserably married. I visited a few women's organisations that were well versed with the abusive behaviour patterns of South-Asian men particularly, and completely understood my story. But there was a certain amount of complacency towards this unhealthy pattern of abuse being inflicted by men on the women in their families. It was the same old story. It was nothing new for the case workers. They had heard various versions of my story many times.

My story is important. It is important not because it is uncommon but because it is not.

There are many such episodes happening behind closed doors of many Canadian homes. Now that I am a women's empowerment coach working one-on-one with immigrant women, I hear horrendous secret stories about women being locked in closets by their men. These women have to be willing to come out of their closets to share their stories for change-makers and law-makers of Canada to see the need for change. A change that would permeate closed doors of many Canadian homes and bring dignity and respect to women. Most of them are afraid to share their stories.

Canada has progressed and we have a gender balanced cabinet since 2015. It is imperative that we create a structure to bring this gender balance behind closed doors of every Canadian home. We need to work towards making gender balance a way of life, a habitual way of thinking, a daily narrative or perhaps a healthy practice between both genders and not just use it as the in-thing to talk about.

One of the ways to ensure progress in this area of life would be to take into consideration that even though verbal violence and emotional abuse is not a crime punishable by law, it does irreparable damage to the wellbeing and complete health of the victims. Most times, these victims are women. Sometimes, it compels them to choose death as an escape. The police are unable to take action if there are no bruises to testify that abuse has taken place. Physical abuse is evident in bruises and injuries that show bodily harm were inflicted. On the other hand, mental, emotional, and verbal abuse leaves untraceable internal scars that are beyond repair and impact their ability to live life fully. Even after the victim's circumstances change for the better, they may show symptoms of Post Traumatic Stress Disorder.

Despite the hush about violence behind closed doors of Canadian homes, in reference to South Asian families particularly, Stats Canada has tabulated a ridiculously un-believable scenario for South Asian women and their re-lationship status in 2009. How far have we progressed in ten years?

The most important observation is that all these be-haviours are often disguised as everyday relationship dy-namics in many homes. I have personally experienced some of these behaviours without ever seeing them as abuse. What may be considered as abuse may perhaps be the normal narrative in many homes. In fact a lot of these behaviours are used to raise well-disciplined children in some homes. These children then grow up to never see themselves being abused because to them it is the way they were raised.

In 2008, in Deepa Mehta's Bollywood film *Heaven on Earth*, Chand is a Punjabi woman from India, who mar-ries an Indo-Canadian man from Brampton, Ontario. She immigrated to Canada and ended up in an abusive mar-riage to eventually succumb under the pressure of abuse. She chooses separation and returns to India. This may be the story of a few immigrant women who came here with dreams of a beautiful future. I personally know of one who secretly pleaded for money from her neighbours and friends in Canada to afford her escape by flight to India. Out of every 1000 women who are sexually abused, only 33 are reported to the police! This ratio has remained al-most the same from 2004 to 2014.[1]

---

1   Statistics Canada, "Section 2: Risk Factors for Violence Against Women," last modified November 30, 2015, https://www150.statcan.gc.ca/n1/pub/85-002-x/2013001/article/11766/11766-2-eng.htm

Just two weeks ago, I watched *Because We are Girls*, a factual entertainment and documentary film at a *Films Changing the World* event at Hot Docs in Toronto. Even in 2019, abuse is still thriving in Canadian homes. People in the family remotely have the capacity to help. Sometimes they do not believe the stories. Even when some women are speaking up or sharing their stories, the perpetrators are getting away because all crimes are not considered crimes.

The laws of the land are not fully equipped to see through the lens of immigrant experiences. In that case, finding solidarity in sharing our stories is the first step towards causing a change. One story at a time, we will bring transformation in Canadian immigrant homes.

Just as every star in the night sky shines its light, we need to shine our lights of experiences and lessons learned. But before that we need to be our own North Stars. We need to access our own guiding force to shine in our own light. In clusters and constellations, one kindle at a time, may we unite to *Lighting the North.* Together.

Chapter Five

ENOUGH

"You are strong. You are soft. You are always enough."

ELDYKA SIMPSON

Eldyka Simpson

French-Canadian | Ukranian | Polish
Russian | Norwegian

www.ripple-effect.ca

ig: @rippleeffectwellness_st.albert | fb: @Ripple Effect
Wellness Centre, St. Albert

Eldyka Simpson is a multifaceted healer and entre-preneur whose eclectic mix of talents and tools have facilitated opportunities for deep healing and transformation in her patients, and eventually led her to build Ripple Effect Wellness Centre, in St. Albert, Alberta.

One part artist, she is a lifetime Honorary Member of the Ukrainian Shumka Dancers; one part healer, she incorporates acupuncture, massage therapy, craniosacral therapy, and energy healing in her clinic practice. A self-proclaimed Birth Warrior, Eldyka clawed her way out of a very deep postpartum depression in large part via her 1000 plus days of intentional (and very public) gratitude journaling. Eldyka cares deeply, and approaches her work with a nurturing and intuitive spirit.

Eldyka is a mother of four, grandmother of two, and wife to a man who she has known since ninth grade. She loves being a dance and hockey mom, and finds joy on the ball diamond, whether as her kids' biggest fan, team manager, or wannabe-shortstop. She loves hanging out with her Soulful Sisters, discussing moon phases, the chakras, the power of nature, and partaking in sacred rituals, and intuitively-guided practices. Eldyka believes in a new paradigm of empowered birth. She believes in building community and authentic connections, and in the innate goodness of people. She believes the Universe provides for each of us abundantly, and she believes strongly, that we are all enough.

Summer 2006, I am expecting my first child. I've been a step-mom for about six years now, but this is my first pregnancy. It has been completely normal—nothing out of the ordinary, and yet, so incredibly extraordinary too. I am growing a baby within, and this miracle hasn't been lost on me. Being under the shared care of a team of midwives has been so empowering. I feel safe within their care, and I am encouraged to find three heart-words to guide me through pregnancy, labor, and birth. These words will become my mantra when I am pushed to the limits of my being and tested in my belief that my body is capable of birthing my baby. I choose CALM, SUPPORTED, and POWERFUL.

July 24, 2006, shortly after midnight. Labor starts quickly with a large gush as my membranes rupture, and immediately, contractions are five minutes apart. I notice a green tinge in the fluid, and before long, there's a lot more. There's no question that meconium is present, and while fairly common in labor, it can be a sign of fetal distress. I call my midwife and she asks us to meet her at the birth centre in Stony Plain, AB. It's actually not a full-fledged birth centre, more a designated wing of the community hospital that is home to the Shared Care Maternity program.

When we arrive, my midwife confirms there is meconium, but reassures me that my baby appears fine on the fetal monitor. I am examined and surprised to learn that I am dilated already to seven centimetres! All the stories I'd heard about first babies taking a long time don't seem to be true for me, and my labor moves quickly. I am reminded to keep my heart-words close. Calm, supported, powerful. Indeed I feel all of these. My body is doing exactly what it needs to be doing.

Despite my quick and easy progress, my midwife explains that she needs to transfer me to the hospital. The meconium is thick and the birth centre isn't equipped for a potential post-birth emergency. Further, because the midwives do not yet have hospital privileges, she must also transfer my care to an obstetrician that I have never met before.

I am devastated at this news. I had chosen midwifery care for many reasons, but the most important to me was the support I would receive when I was at my most vulnerable. How would I ever be supported, calm, and powerful when I was about to be transferred to a medical staff that I'd never met before and to a hospital setting I'd never imagined? I had really counted on delivering in the birthing tub with my midwife, husband, and stepdaughter all holding space around me. It really is an unfortunate reality that most birth stories that we hear about are filled with fear and trauma, and I had really expected an experience different than the ones I had heard from so many friends and family.

Although I trust my midwife, my heart breaks as I am loaded into the ambulance and transferred to the nearest hospital, in the back of a screeching ambulance. Quite possibly the world's youngest paramedic is with me; he seems incredibly nervous, and keeps telling me they will have to pull over if I start to push. He recognizes that this baby could be born at any minute now, and I long to have him put his stopwatch down and just put his hand on my shoulder. I feel so very alone.

My husband and stepdaughter will be at the hospital, but my midwife will not be in attendance. It will be three more years before midwives are fully integrated into the labor and delivery systems here in Alberta, and I'm acutely aware that I am a stranger to everyone on the ward; they are a stranger to me. I've been laboring beautifully and remembering my midwife Noreen's gentle wisdom, "Trust your body, trust your baby."

It is nearly six in the morning, an hour before shift change. The nurse checks me and I am still seven centimetres dilated. Funny how stress can slow things down. But a progressive labor doesn't stall for long, and a short time later I know that I have to push.

The nurse is called and when she peeks around the door, she says, "Oh, Honey, you were just seven centimetres—trust me you don't need to push yet."

And just like that, *POP*!

The bubble that my midwife had built around me for thirty eight weeks—this bubble of trusting my intuition, trusting my body, trusting my baby—explodes. *What do I know? How stupid to think I need to push already. Who am I to believe that my first labor could indeed be short and easy? How will I actually know when it's time to push now, if my body has betrayed me already?*

My husband is constant in his support for me, and reminds me of my strength. I carry on, following my instincts, my body doing this divine work of birthing my baby. I find myself on my knees at the end of the bed, arms hanging around my husband's neck. My stepdaughter is observing, quietly holding space in the way only an innocent nine year old can.

Thirty minutes later, my body is pushing on its own, without any extra effort from me. Yet the nurse offers no checks, no reassurance. "I'll send the doctor in shortly; she's just finishing up in another room."

Just before seven o'clock, the doctor enters and says, "I'm off in ten minutes, but apparently you need to push. You were only seven centimetres though, so I will check you again and pass you on to the next doctor." *She'll pass me on, like I'm some sort of possession. She'll pass me on, at this point at her shift's end, like I'm a nuisance.*

As she preps for the check, she berates my midwife (again, not in attendance) for sending me in because "there are no signs of meconium and the midwife clearly doesn't know what she's doing." I work hard to stay in my zone. The doctor forces me from my comfortable hands-and-knees position into the convenient-for-her position on my back. She checks me and starts to bellow, "Well the head is right here, why didn't you tell anyone? Start pushing! No don't push like that! Don't make a sound! No you can't be on your hands and knees! Nurse, hold her leg and make sure she is silent!"

Despite the unwelcome barrage of instructions, I am proud of the fact that indeed I did know my body; I did have to push, just like I had said. I push through the next contraction, three pushes, ten seconds each, being told each time not to moan, but to hold my breath instead. As the wave subsides, the doctor steps back in and declares that because I hadn't told anyone that my baby was so low, she could be losing oxygen right now so we'll have to do a vacuum.

"*NO!*" I scream, and land a kick to her shoulder as she approaches with this cold sterile tool. I fight against the constraints of the nurse and resident, each holding a limb, and yet, against my consent, the doctor applies the vacuum. On the very next contraction, at 7:05 a.m., she pulls my baby out of me.

There is a flurry of activity at this point. A nurse is checking my baby, to ensure that she is breathing. I wait impatiently to hold her skin-to-skin. I am crying, so is my husband. All the emotions. We have a baby, a daughter. She is perfectly pink, perfectly healthy—in no way harmed by the thick meconium of a few hours ago.

I am transformed. I am a mother.

The influx of friends and family over the next few days gives me the chance to tell my story many times. "At least she's healthy," is the common refrain. "At least you didn't have to have a Cesarean like so-and-so," others say. "At least your labor wasn't twenty-four hours long—that is how long I suffered," lamented others who, without meaning too, implied that the trauma I experienced was somehow less than theirs.

Part of me wants to scream, "Yes, of course I'm glad she's healthy and that labor was short, but did you hear the part when I was mistreated? Where they forced themselves on me and used the vacuum without my consent?" It astounds me that almost no one thinks it matters. No one asks me how I am. Despite being so in love with this little one, I am so hurt, so sad, so angry.

How dare they tell me that I wasn't good enough to know my baby, to know my body? How dare they go against my consent and pull my baby from me, when I was doing a fine job of birthing her on my own just minutes before? How dare I be given the very clear message that I was NOT STRONG ENOUGH to birth my own baby and NOT WORTHY ENOUGH to step into motherhood in a way that was calm, supported, and powerful?

Innately, I know this is something I don't need to accept. In these early days after my daughter's birth, I myself was reborn. I don the unwritten title of Birth Warrior, and am fueled with a deep desire to ensure that no woman is disrespected in birth again.

In the fourteen years since my daughter's birth, I have supported hundreds of women in my clinic and in their births. I have witnessed women learning to trust their bodies to conceive and grow their babies perfectly, and learning to birth their babies from that same inner trust. I have learned that the human species is the only one that questions their ability to birth, and so often it's starting from a global, systemic, deeply-ingrained belief of *not-enough-ness*. I believe fully that this needs to change, right from the way we speak of pregnancy and birth to our young girls, to the way birthing persons are spoken to in birth itself.

In the fourteen years since I became a mother, I have witnessed birth from two very distinct angles: one of fear, and one of trust. I have heard degrading comments from nurses and doctors; a lack of consent; and fear tactics that do nothing but disempower.[1]

In the fourteen years since I was reborn anew, I have held space for many women afterwards sharing their stories of shame that their bodies didn't do the right thing in birth. I have built my practice for all women, not only physically helping their symptoms with acupuncture and energy work, but also supporting them emotionally and spiritually as they move through their very personal journey from maiden to mother. It has been noted that one's satisfaction in a birthing experience is associated with criteria such as supportive and considerate treatment by medical caregivers, along with emotional support (from caregivers, birth attendants, and partners), physical support (in whatever way the birthing person needs), and informational support required to participate in decision-making throughout the experience.[2]

---

1   Simkin, Penny. "Just Another Day in a Woman's Life? Women's Long-Term Perception of Their First Birth Experience. Part 1." *Birth 18* (December 1991): 203-210, https://doi.org/10.1111/j.1523-536X.1991.tb00103.x

2   Hodnett, Ellen D, Simon Gates, Justus G. Hofmeyer, and Carol Sakala. "Continuous Support During Childbirth," *Cochrane Database* Syst Rev. (October 2012): http://doi.org/10.1002/14651858.CD003766.pub4

I have learned that the stories of not-enoughness don't just start in pregnancy and birth, and they certainly don't end there either. Much of the work I do with these patients hinges around unravelling the decades of learned mistrust in themselves, the shame they feel for their soft hearts and bellies, and the disconnect they have from their true powers. It is at once, astounding and so very disheartening to see how and where this theme of, "not enough" exists. It exists within the very fabric of almost every woman I've met over the past fourteen years. It exists when she is sitting with her baby, wondering how she can make it through another sleepless night, worried that she is not doing enough, not being enough, unable to meet the breastfeeding needs of her baby and the all-encompassing needs of her toddler. It exists as the mama struggles to fill all the roles she carries in her home—mother, wife, cook, seamstress, educator, and chauffeur.

Outside of the home, this "not enough-ness" exists in the professional woman told she cannot have the job at the engineering firm because she isn't strong enough mentally to compete with the big boys. It exists with the teenager who feels she will never live up to Instagram's portrayal of how she should look and wonders how she can be *liked* more. It exists in the playgrounds and ball fields, where "running like a girl" and "throwing like a girl" are tossed around like insults, insinuating that she just isn't as good or as strong or as capable as the boys.

I was a confident child and felt strong in my capabilities. Yet when I began the journey to regain my wholeness, I realized that my own journey with not-enoughness still started at a very young age. I was the young girl who could never please her grandfather. We didn't visit enough; our Catholic faith was made a mockery; he offered to pay for my post-secondary education, but only if I became a teacher or a *real* doctor; apparently Chinese medicine wasn't good enough. *Nothing was ever enough.*

I was a dancer and administrator who poured herself into every facet of an organization (presidency, running the dance school, diving head-first into character roles, instructing for decades). In 2009, I was awarded a prestigious award for my work, and a couple days later got a call from my male colleague, one of my best friends at the time, not to congratulate me, but rather to ask me, "Well, what are you going to do with the award now? How will you make a difference now?" *As if the eighteen years of work I did to receive the award in the first place wasn't good enough to stand on its own.*

I was the new mom who heard one of my closest friends sing a beautiful lullaby to my baby, and then follow it up with, "Don't get used to that Baby; your Mama doesn't sing well." *How dare she tell me I'm not good enough to sing to my own baby?!*

When I started to write this story, my daughter was twelve, and she believed she could do anything. She threw herself into every sport and game in phys-ed, believing fully she could compete with the boys. She believed she could dress as she pleased and be accepted for who she was, as she was. She put her hand up in class, unafraid to appear *too smart* or *too eager*, and she never hesitated to say *YES* when there's something she wanted, and *NO* when something didn't feel quite right. She's wise, this one. At the age of ten, she left a message on an easel at my clinic, written in small, colourful magnetic letters.

CALM. BOLD. I AM ENOUGH.

When she created it, I was momentarily stunned, and asked her where she learned the words. "From you, Mom" and I was so overcome with emotion and gratitude. There was such a deep sense of relief knowing that everything I had ever experienced had happened so that this very moment with my daughter could happen too.

In all honesty, I see parts of her self-belief eroding and small snippets of self-doubt creeping in. While I know it's a normal and necessary ritual to go through as she grows, it makes my mama-heart sad to know that I haven't been able to protect her from this raging epidemic of not enough-ness. She will likely find herself grappling with it as she moves through these tender years of junior high and I can only hope that she will stay true to her strong powerful self more easily than I did. At forty-five years of age, I'm just starting to scratch that surface, and man, does it ever feel good when I'm standing in the abundant flow and glow of all the enoughness that I am. I long to not worry whatsoever about what others think and to live life in a way that is deeply caring to others while deeply authentic to myself. I have learned, and continue to learn, that I am enough. I am smart enough; I work hard enough; I accomplish enough; I am pretty enough; I am strong enough to push through challenges; and soft enough to surrender and trust what is.

In Chinese Medicine, we look at the theory of Yin-Yang as a guiding principle in our diagnosis and treatment protocols. At its simplest, Yin-Yang (which most recognize as the black-and-white symbol that adorns many a cheap souvenir or an inked arm) represents the duality that exists in every single thing in the Universe. Male and female. Hot and cold. Sun and moon. Strong and soft. Neither of these extremes can exist without the other, and over time, they become each other. Night becomes day; day becomes night. We don't have to force anything and we trust the process implicitly. We wouldn't know the brilliance of light if we never experienced the depth of dark. We couldn't know the strength of character if we didn't experience the surrender of the soul.

In my mind, birth is the epitome of Yin-Yang theory. Going into labor itself and every single contraction is the hard work of Yang, bringing the birthing person to the place where they don't know if they can go on. The space between contractions is Yin, where we see the surrender-ing, the softening, the opening up to receive, the trusting the body to do its divine work. Neither Yin nor Yang is more important than the other. In fact, each is absolutely necessary. When we give up the deeply-ingrained need to control and our deeply-ingrained self-limiting beliefs, we ironically often find the most progress in birth. I am hon-ored to have been invited into the very intimate world of birth as a doula, where I have witnessed women showing undoubtedly their full strength and raw power in their full go-get-em energy of Yang, complemented completely by the gracious, spacious energy of Yin, where they fully let go and soften to receive their babies.

Strong and soft. What a perfect combination for birth; what a perfect combination for life.

My dream is that every birthing woman knows that they are capable and powerful, that they are supported, that their voice matters. My dream is that every girl grows to know her worth and fully expects to be accepted for who she is. My dream is that every woman knows that she is strong, she is soft, and she is always enough.

You are enough.

SUSAN MUSGRAVE

https://www.susanmusgrave.com

Empty Benches in Snow

I pass by, high above the sea, not stopping
to discover the names of the dead
each cold bench commemorates. The snow
is what I like best about these
empty benches. It covers the old names
with the tenderness of an old mother
under a hard winter sky called remembering.

Chapter Six

DAANIS

"Your soul compass knows the way."

CRYSTAL HARDY ZONGWE BINESIKWE

Crystal Hardy Zongwe Binesikwe

Biinjitiwaabik Zaaging Anishinaabek First Nation

www.zongwebinesikwe.com

Crystal "Zee" Hardy is an Anishinaabe hand drummer from Biinjitiwaabik Zaaging Anishinaabek in Northern Ontario. Her Spirit name is Zongwe Binesikwe (Sounding Thunderbird Woman). She is the host of *Under the Same Stars* podcast and Zee's Place radio show on CILU Radio. Crystal shares her knowledge and experience as a Nurse Practitioner and PhD in Nursing Candidate at Queen's University with her personal healing journey as an Indigenous woman in Canada. She makes thunder in keynote addresses and seminars with topics related to decolonizing healthcare practices through cultural humility, empowerment of Indigenous people, and missing and murdered Indigenous women in Canada.

To you, dear reader, chi-miigwetch (thank you so much) for holding space for me to share a small part of myself. I am Zongwe Binesikwe, which is Anishinaabe (Ojibwe) for Sounding Thunderbird Woman. My English name is Crystal Hardy. As my life combines both Indigenous and Western ways of knowing, you will notice Anishinaabe (Ojibwe) words followed by the English translation. This chapter is dedicated to my daanis (daughter), Evelyn, who continues to teach me so much every single day.

Daanis: A Letter to my Daughter

Dear Daanis (Daughter),

Chi-miigwetch (thank you so much) for choosing me as your mama. I am so blessed to have you in my life. I write this letter to you in hopes that it will help you understand me and how intergenerational trauma has affected our lives. This is my perception of the events in my life and how I was able to break the cycle of disadvantage in our family. My greatest wish has been to protect you from the things that hurt me growing up, while helping you flourish into a powerful human being. So, as in our oral traditions, let me tell you my story through the lens of our medicine wheel teachings.

The medicine wheel guides us to live in balance through the teachings of the four directions. The wheel, or circle represents the connectedness of all things in life. The medicine wheel is divided into four coloured quadrants (yellow, red, black and white) that acknowledge the cycles of our lives, such as the directions, seasons, and stages of life. Let's begin in the East, where all life begins . . .

WABUNNOONG (EAST)

On a warm autumn day in northern Ontario, I became a daanis to a beautiful, young couple. Weighing just over five pounds, I was born small, feisty and early—Zongwe Binesikwe wasn't going to wait any longer to make thunder. I chose these beautiful humans to be my first parents. Traditionally, all members of the community would raise a child—so we would have many parents to help shape our development. Although they tried to create a loving home for me, their own relationship quickly deteriorated. They separated when I was still an infant and I spent most of my childhood with my mother.

To illustrate intergenerational trauma and give context to the events in my childhood, we first need to learn about my mother (another daanis). My mom was the only girl in the family of four children. She said that she felt that her mother never wanted her. She felt unworthy of love, so she moved on her own at the age of seventeen. Then I was born. After my parents separated, my mother moved from one abusive relationship to the next. She experienced all types of abuse in her life at the hands of family, friends, and partners. She would tell me stories of her past abuses that I did not fully understand. As with many people who struggle with trauma, she sought escape through drugs and alcohol. These substances provided short relief from the thoughts of unworthiness.

After my little sister was born, we moved across the country with my mother's boyfriend. He promised her a fresh start. When we arrived, her boyfriend continued to abuse her. My mom did her best to protect us, but eventually we had to pack our bags and leave in the middle of the night to escape a hostile situation. This cycle continued to repeat with her future relationships. Although these events lessened after my brother was born, we continued to be on the move. Throughout my childhood, I attended more than forty schools. I didn't bother trying to make friends because I knew we would be on the move within a month again. My mother did her best to raise her three children—and utilized me as a friend, co-parent, and confidante. She found means to secure food—including the use of food banks and shelters. She secured funds through theft, drug trafficking, and eventually sex trafficking. There were many days that my mother would be gone, either procuring or spending money. During this time, I would send my sister to school and stay home to care for my baby brother. This did not seem out of the ordinary, as many families in our neighbourhood did the same. My mother struggled with coping with her past and her present situations. When she was home, she would use intravenous drugs and be awake and paranoid for long periods of time. Then she would sleep on the floor for what felt like many days without waking. I would tend to her and make sure she was breathing, while offering her water and small bites of food. Then she would wake, clean the house, get food from the food bank, spend time with us, and the cycle would begin again. As time passed, we were placed into the foster care system. This was one of the most difficult events in my life. I was nine years old and did not understand why we were removed from our home.

ZHAAWANONG (SOUTH)

It was a warm, spring day in British Columbia when I became the daanis to my second parents. They cared for me and my siblings like their own children. I had a really difficult time giving up my maternal role and fought my foster mother all the way. She wanted me to be a kid that didn't have to worry and could play and have fun. Finally, I gave in. I started to read many books and create arts and crafts, which are things that I still enjoy today. During this time, my mother continued to decline. She would miss many visits and ultimately did not show at all. I recall many weekends sitting on the stairs looking out the front door. I would wait for hours, and then cry in my room when I realized she wasn't coming. I yearned for my mother's love and wanted to return to my family home. This made me feel unworthy of love and needed ways to protect my heart from future heartbreak. Although I was in a loving home, I didn't quite feel like part of the family, or that I deserved to be loved. I yearned to belong, but always felt like I didn't really fit. I reconnected with my dad, which led to my relocation to Ontario to live with my grandparents. I was closer to my dad, but separated from my siblings. It was so difficult, but my instincts were pulling me back to my roots. Unfortunately, living with my grandparents was short lived. As you can imagine, I had many emotional difficulties at this time. I was moving into my teenage years and had never really understood the effects of trauma. I had a hard time in my new school and other children teased me. I couldn't understand why my father couldn't care for me. I missed my mother and my siblings. I continued to feel isolated and fell into a deep depression. I locked myself in my room and contemplated suicide for many days. Thankfully, when my head was screaming lies, my heart showed me the truth. I needed a change and was placed back into foster care.

NINGAABI'ANONG (WEST)

It was an early summer afternoon when I became the daanis within a great, loving foster family. Unconditional love was a big teaching in our home—since unconditional love is created through conditions. Even though they always accepted me as one of their own children, I would run away (physically and emotionally). I tried to numb my feelings with drugs and alcohol, while pushing away anyone that might try to see past my protective armour. It took a suspension from school to realize that I was starting down the path that might lead me in the same fate as my mother. I made a conscious decision to change my future. I distanced myself from most of my friends and focused on my school studies. I learned about faith, love, and trust. I saw how unhealthy my past was. My foster family continues to teach me about the importance of family and roots and helped build my connection to my faith and spirituality; I am so grateful that they love and support me every day!

GIIWEDINONG (NORTH)

I am a daanis (daughter) of the Creator, God, the Universe. It was a crisp, winter evening in northern Ontario, when I reconnected to the Creator. I felt something inside me pulling for something more than money or success. I needed love—the love from others and the Creator, but most importantly for myself. This has been the most difficult part of my journey—self-love. The traumas from my childhood have really affected my confidence and feelings of self-worth. My mother often punished me for crying or speaking up. Throughout my healing work, I uncovered a heavily repressed memory of sexual trauma from my childhood. My mother denied that it happened and to not talk about it. These actions led to my inability to trust myself, my intuition, my soul's compass. Reconnecting with the Creator has helped me remember and live my truth. I realized my protective armour was shielding me from connecting fully to His divinity. Now I see and acknowledge the messages He sends me through Spirit in people, music, animals, in everything! This healing journey has not been an easy one, but I'm worth all of this hard work—and so are you!

TO MY DAANIS (DAUGHTER)

Chi-miigwetch (thank you so much) again for choosing me as your mother. You are my most valued teacher. You have shown me that childhood should be filled with innocence, security, and love. You teach me about seeing the beauty and joy in life's simple treasures. That love and light is in all things and we need only take a moment to see it! I will continue to work at being the best version of myself for you, for me, and for all our relations! Never forget, my beautiful Daanis, your soul compass knows the way.

MISS EMILY

German | Hessian | British | Scandanavian
www.themissemily.com
t & ig: @themissemily | fb: @themissemilymusic
photo: Jillian Lorraine Photography

Prince Edward County born, full-time musician Miss Emily has called Kingston, Ontario home now for sixteen years. Her latest album *In Between* featuring Gord Sinclair & Rob Baker from The Tragically Hip has garnered much interest from the blues community, for which she is very grateful. Miss Emily is a three time Maple Blues Award nominee and the 2019 winner of New Artist of the Year and Female Vocalist of the Year. Emily performs at festivals and concert halls in Canada, the U.S., the U.K., and Europe. She is a long-time passionate supporter of many charities, especially the Light Of Day Foundation which raises money for Parkinson's Disease Research.

* * *

I grew up in a small rural community in Southern Ontario. It's called Prince Edward County, otherwise known as "The County." It is familiar to the provincial tourists who love sandy beaches and adorable small villages and towns, connected by rural roads along farm fields. It was a beautiful place to grow up. Small schools, small class sizes, knowing all of your neighbours (being related to many of them too!), and popular community events like the strawberry social and the village fair (not the kind with rides). *Note: This was the 1980s and 90s, not the 1880s and 90s.*

The village near where I lived was Milford, a hamlet really, in the south end of the county. Perhaps sixty or so folks lived within the village limits and the rest of us were spread out over farm fields dotted with family homes.

And everyone was white.

Truth. I believe there were two or three Chinese families (possibly more) in the entire county, but where I grew up, there were only white people. My entire elementary school, Kindergarten to Grade 8—white. There were two little schools down the road from each other; the single hallway school had Kindergarten to Grade 4; and Grades 5 to 8 were in the two hallway schools in nearby Cherry Valley. To my recollection, everyone was white. Teachers, custodians, students . . . It's possible there were some people in my school who had more diverse backgrounds, but I guess that's the beauty of children; they really don't see colour. At least I don't remember seeing colour. I didn't think of my classmates as being all white, I just thought of them as my classmates.

I can imagine it must have been difficult for my county-born-and-raised parents to talk about race relations and white privilege with me when we didn't have people of colour around to whom to relate the issues. But somehow, in that upbringing, I learned about Harriet Tubman and the Underground Railroad, which lead to learning about slavery, which lead to me asking questions about the many black musicians and singers we listened to in our home.

There is NO WAY I learned enough about black history to make myself some sort of scholar on the topic, but I did learn some. Probably more than many of my peers. I was lucky that way. Education is a right, but specific education like the history of Indigenous, black, and other people of colour seems to be a privilege. *Note: I realize by just writing that sentence that our school curriculum needs to change and we need to not only include more of this specific history, but FOCUS on this specific history.*

To give credit where it is due (and with no disrespect to my parents' efforts) the bulk of my education on race relations came from *Oprah*. True story. She was on at 4:00 pm every weekday and the bus dropped me off in the driveway just in time to grab a snack and turn on the TV to see what she had to say. This is where I learned about the injustice that was plaguing so much of the black community in North America. She had guests on her show that had stories to tell (mostly sad and heartbreaking) about their treatment in society as African Americans. It was eye-opening to me and I cried. A lot. She was pure magic in how she shaped conversations with guests and audience members. She spoke passionately about issues in the world, especially race related issues. Although I couldn't fully put myself in the shoes of someone of colour, I learned to at least acknowledge that I couldn't do that and it was my responsibility to try and educate other white people on the injustices that were overwhelming the black community.

And in the way a child can, I tried. After watching and re-watching a specific episode of *Oprah* centred around the Little Rock Nine, I decided I would write an informative speech on the event and use it at the annual school board public speaking contest. I was so moved by this story and I was sure others would be too. *Note: If you don't know what the Little Rock Nine refers to, it refers to the nine black students who enrolled in Little Rock Central High School in 1957. Their enrollment caused an uprising in Little Rock and the Governor of Arkansas called in the National Guard to prevent them from attending classes on the first day of school. I highly encourage you to research it. Find that Oprah episode (there may even have been two!) if you can. This is an important piece of history. Not just black history, but human history. Across the board, this is an amazing story of heartbreak and courage.*

There were only two of us in the fourteen-year-old category. Apparently public speaking wasn't an exciting activity for that age demographic. But I had something to say! I wanted to do something that I thought was proactive in making the world a better place, not just for people of colour, but for ultimately everyone.

I lost the public speaking contest to the other participant. Her speech was about her messy bedroom. Apparently, my insistence on trying to educate the audience about this piece of history made people uncomfortable. People don't like to be uncomfortable and people really don't like to feel uncomfortable at the hands of a child. My dad was mad. I was confused. I wasn't a poor loser, but I knew my speech was better. It was researched. It was informative. But ultimately, it made that very, very white room uncomfortable.

As an adult, I still see that it is uncomfortable to talk about racial issues, and sadly because we absorb these moments and experiences as children, I have grown to be an adult who does not often talk about racial issues. At least not in a public forum. I started working with my daughter when she was a toddler, teaching her about white privilege and racial injustices, but those conversations didn't really go beyond our home life.

I am a full-time soul musician. I sing, I write, I play soul-blues music. The backbone, foundation, and history of the music from which I make a living is rooted in the black community. Without their contributions, I would not have a career in music; plain and simple. To say I am indebted to the black community is only the tip of the iceberg of my gratitude, and I have a hard time expressing it in words. I cannot relate to the experiences from which this music was born. I do know that it has moved me, it has defined me, and it has compelled me to make it my life's work. Perhaps I am due for some more research and reflection on why this music is so unique and special. It's a step in the right direction, anyway, of appreciating and acknowledging some of the great contributions of black culture.

In closing, I'd just like to say that we all have a place in making our society a safer, more appreciative place for black people and people of colour. We cannot change the past, but it wouldn't hurt to apologise for it. We also have the opportunity to acknowledge the injustices currently plaguing marginalized communities and to educate ourselves as white people on what is wrong, why it is wrong and what we can do to help make changes that will fix these issues. We owe it to people of colour, our next generation of children, and to ourselves. We all benefit from unity and peace.

This piece is dedicated to George Floyd and the thousands of people of colour who have lost their lives unjustly at the hands of a broken and ignorant society. It is also dedicated to the many people currently making it their lives' work to improve racial injustice in our world. #blacklivesmatter

Chapter Seven

STUCK IN THE MIDDLE

"I've felt the facing and invisibility of being mixed race, and also of being middle class."

SASHA ROSE

Sasha Rose

First Nations | Inuit | Chinese | Scottish
English | French
ig: @sasharose_4 | @theroseregrowth
fb: @sasharose4

Sasha Rose is a woman with big ideas and dreams. She learned from her mother and two sisters that when you have an idea, you put it into action and see it through. Sasha is the Assistant Publisher for Golden Brick Road Publishing House, a hospitality entrepreneur, with her most recent venture has been pairing up with her sister to create Oneida Grand Centre and Bistro (located South of Ottawa, Ontario).

Sasha has always wanted to be a mother, and has been gifted with the ever challenging and rewarding title of mama to her two daughters. She hopes to find a way to make a small difference in this world for her girls to grow up safe and confident.

Sasha is a spiritual woman and an avid animal and outdoor lover. She strives for the life she has always wanted; to own a hobby farm with her family. Sasha is currently working toward her 200-hour yoga teacher certification to heal herself and others. Sasha comes from a mixed background including Scottish, English, and French on her mother's side, and First Nations, Inuit, and Chinese on her father's side.

As a young, mixed-race woman born and raised in Canada, I still do not know how to relate to the word "Canadian." What exactly does that mean? What does it mean to you? Does it mean you love maple syrup and plaid jackets? Because I do. Do you have beavers and moose wandering through your streets? Not in my hometown. When do you begin to prep your igloo for the Winter? Growing up on the West Coast of British Columbia I could barely accomplish building a snowman because of the lack of snow, let alone an igloo. All of these are stereotypes and do not apply to every person living in Canada, we are not all living in a comedy.

Do you feel strong and free? Do you feel healthy and cared for? Depending on job title, status, ancestry, or skin colour, I often wonder how most Canadians feel.

Or does it simply mean being born in Canada? If that is the case, then what about all the immigrants who reside within our country? And most importantly, what about the Indigenous people who owned this land before it was called Canada?

I am a thirty-year-old mother of two with multicultural blood flowing through me; Scottish, English, and French-Canadian on my mother's side; and First Nations, Inuit, and Chinese on my father's side. Yet, I was raised "white" and "Canadian," to say it was anything but confusing would be an understatement. As a child, it was a joke that my sisters and I were "mutts." It was easier to laugh it off than have an open discussion about where my family came from and the hardships they (most definitely) faced. Growing up, as my *friends* learned of my heritage, they instantly felt it was okay to speak racial slurs around me, or speak in condescending accents that mimicked those of my ancestors. But still, I laughed it off because everyone else laughed, I knew it was wrong, but didn't know how to tell them to stop.

I have been kept in the shadows (not intentionally by my family) from experiencing this side of me because when my (Indigenous) great grandfather needed to find work to support his family, he had his status ripped away from him. Furthermore, when my Indigenous grandmother married my (non-biological) white grandfather, she was unable to obtain her status. Having an Indigenous grandmother and a white grandfather did not seem odd to me because I had an Indigenous father and a white mother. I did not know my grandfather was not blood related until my adult years, I was completely naive to this. My grandparents' house did not have any culture to it; no Indigenous artwork or music, no stories of our family's past, no cultural food. Their house was like our house, and all my white friend's houses, so I never inquired.

The most confusing part of my heritage and being raised as a white girl has been my instinctual pull toward, what I feel to be, my First Nations heritage; my love for the earth and all its creatures led to being labelled a "hippy" within my group of friends; you can often find me openly thanking the trees for their beauty, or wildlife for choosing to walk across my path. I now proudly embrace this part of myself. I still remember visiting a long house on Vancouver Island for a field trip as a child and it was magical, my soul felt happy while I was there, but that was a one time encounter that I long to experience again. Now, I realize one does not need to be Indigenous to be spiritual or to love mother Earth, but for me, I feel that is where my love for nature comes from.

Over the last ten years or so, I often wondered why there are so many labels in our society. Why do people feel the need to question "What are you?" There are the labels to establish status; stay-at-home-mom, lawyer, labourer, Red Seal mechanic (not just a backyard mechanic), or someone on disability. This type of label identifies us to the banks, to our friends, and gains us employment. And then there are the labels specifically to do with our skin colour, beliefs, or heritage—this forces much judgement within our society; White, Asian, Indigenous, European, Black, etc. Why can't I just be a human, a woman? Why must it change someone's view of me because of my employment or where my family came from? I've always been intrigued, and upset by this because it makes me feel like a box to check off, just another number on a census form or a government document. Maybe I feel emotional toward this topic because I don't exactly know *what* I am, and society has ingrained it into me that I must know. I found this a lot in my twenties, specifically when speaking to men when I was single, they were curious to know *what* to refer to me as—my name is Sasha, refer to me as that.

Many would lead a conversation with, "You are so different looking, what are you?" This always came from white men and really bothered me . . . what about me makes me so different? I am visibly white, with features that represent my heritage; fair skin, blue eyes, with freckles and blonde highlights (in summertime) represent my white heritage; high cheekbones, thick dark hair, and easily tanning skin represent my Indigenous heritage; and slightly folded eyelids represent my Chinese heritage. Some of these features have been passed along to my daughters. My oldest with fair skin, freckles, blonde hair, and blue eyes, and my youngest with olive skin, slightly folded eyelids, dirty blonde hair, and brown eyes. I don't want them to be judged as an outsider for inquiring about their heritage because they don't look "enough" like one nationality or the other. Shouldn't it be enough that they are happy, healthy children? Can't our society come to terms with the fact that we are all "mixed" to some degree? That the majority of Canadian residents are immigrants, unless you are of Indigenous descent—and even so, many Nations have been blended for centuries now.

I have spent my life in the middle of cultures, but also within the middle of the Canadian economic landscape. I've felt the facing and invisibility of being mixed race, and also of being middle class. Living in British Columbia was a struggle as a young, working parent; high rents, high grocery costs, and even higher gas prices. I have always strived to be independent and have done my best to earn a good wage to support my family; I opted for work experience, rather than racking up a high student loan debt.

Sasha Rose

Minimum wage in British Columbia has been increased to $14.60 per hour,[1] yet the minimum income needed to live in the province, let's take Victoria (the province's capital) for example, is $19.39.[2] How on earth is someone supposed to work for close to $5.00 per hour less than the minimum needed and survive? How is anyone, especially Millennials (born between 1980 and 1994), expected to get ahead? To become homeowners? To support their parents as they get older? To pay for post-secondary school for themselves or their (future) children? The pressure on this generation to be "material rich" is overwhelming. If you don't have a nice car or house (and post it all on social media), you are somewhat looked down on by those more successful or "insta-happy" than you. It's not new news that the Canadian society is suffering, that a huge part of our country is struggling paycheque-to-paycheque and living at, or below, the poverty line.[3] Some may look like they have it all—nice car, good house, clean clothes—but the reality is, they are likely drowning in debt, gasping for air each time a deposit swiftly enters and exits their bank account. I, as a mother with two children full time who is recently separated, feel like I'm drowning in debt. Before

1   "Minimum Wage," Gov.bc.ca (website), last updated June 1, 2020, https://www2.gov.bc.ca/gov/content/employment-business/employment-standards-advice/employment-standards/wages/minimum-wage

2   "Living Wages in BC and Canada," Living Wage for Families Campaign (website), last updated July, 2019, http://www.livingwageforfamilies.ca/living_wage_rates

3   "B.C. Poverty Reduction," Gov.bc.ca (website), accessed July 14, 2020, https://engage.gov.bc.ca/bcpovertyreduction/poverty-reduction-101/#:~:text=Using%20the%20Market%20Basket%20Measure,four%20about%20%2440%2C000%20a%20year

my new job and marriage, I was thousands of dollars (annually) below the poverty line, and all I was paying for then was half the cost of a rental house, and my basic needs.

Being middle class means the appearance of living comfortably; from time-to-time my family had extra money for toys or meals out, but not without checking the bank account first to make sure the banking juggle act could live another day. Being a middle class, married couple, on paper we looked to have a decent income—falling within the bracket of the middle class[4]—so we were approved for two new vehicles and we figured we could manage it. *The bank said we could, so we must be able to!* But looping loans in with high (unavoidable) rent, the annual costs of moving due to rentals frequently selling, BC Hydro, high gas prices and grocery costs, we were cruising on a sinking ship as the financial stress piled on.

Now, I can't really complain about our vehicles because nobody forced us into signing on the dotted line, but we also needed something reliable to drive. We shopped for older vehicles through the dealerships, the ones with the $10,000 price tags, not the $30,000 to $70,000, but unfortunately banks do not offer loans for older vehicles, and we couldn't go any longer with the ones we had—we didn't have a nest egg to rely on for the repairs they required—so we were presented with "manageable" payments for brand new vehicles. The criteria for meeting a loan application through a dealership for a brand new car

---

4   Stephanie Hogan, "Who is Canada's Middle Class?" CBC News (website), posted October 13, 2019, https://www.cbc.ca/news/politics/canada-votes-2019-middle-class-trudeau-scheer-definition-1.5317206

is way too simple. They manage to fudge the numbers to appease the bank, and don't take into account trying to save as a young family, or for emergencies. Every extra dollar we had went to paying these gargantuan loans.

I may look like I am doing fine, but I have debt up to my eyeballs and I don't even own my home. I do not have "family money" to rely on to purchase a home, so that my monthly bills are dropped—because the cost of renting is outrageous now. We moved amongst some of the smallest coastal towns in British Columbia because the rent was a tad bit less than the city, and we commuted for work. For perspective, we rented a 1400 square foot, over one-hundred-year-old house, with uninsulated floors and a leaky basement for $1,850 per month (utilities not included). Factoring in this rent, plus budgeting a minimum of $300 per month for utilities ($500 in the winter), cost of fuel at $120 per week to commute to work or the bigger grocery stores, and $500 (conservitavely) per month for groceries for my family, there goes my salary. This doesn't even take into account my vehicle payments and insurance, cue my spouse's income to help with that.

So how is a single, working parent supposed to get by with the inflation on housing, groceries, and gas? How many people stay in an unhappy marriage or at an un-fulfilling job just because of debt? How many amazingly talented people do we have in our society that could be beneficial to our country, but never had the chance because of a capitalist system that sees them as disposable? I know people who are talented in the trades, cooking, or in music, but since they do not have a college or university certificate or degree, or money in the bank to start their own business, they go unnoticed within our society.

I am a mother who chooses to work full-time, am an entrepreneur to aim to get ahead, pay my taxes, and I feel as though I am lost in the cracks of society. I have chosen to take a second job in starting a business with my sister, this has been a lifelong dream of ours. When COVID-19 hit in March 2020, a global pandemic that shut down the world, I was luckier than many, but in a position where my second job was weeks away from starting—then became months—and it was extra income I was relying on (and still do). If you had two jobs and lost one during the pandemic, your income could be cut in half, but since you still held a job, you didn't qualify for the government funding (CERB: Canadian Emergency Response Benefit[5]). This *benefit* provided those who lost all employment with $2000 taxable income per month. I'm sorry, but who can live off of that amount per month? This is far less than a full-time minimum wage income—forget about getting ahead. Payment deferrals (loans and mortgages) were incredibly helpful during the first few months of the pandemic, but you had to have a total loss of income to qualify. This pandemic has shown us how many people are living beyond their means and struggling in doing so. I am talking about basic needs, not luxury; a safe rental (not a dive), having a safe vehicle with a warranty, buying a new car seat, and buying fresh vegetables. I can rarely seek medical

---

5   "Canada Emergency Response Benefit (CERB)," Government of Canada (website), last modified June 23, 2020, https://www.canada.ca/en/services/benefits/ei/cerb-application.html

assistance (chiropractor, massage, eyecare, dental) when needed because it may overdraw my account before my benefits kick in and pay back; and I am incredibly fortunate to even have benefits, which so many go without in our society.

Being in a position within society where finding a second source of income is a struggle for many; even taking a raise or promotion has its cons. You must take into consideration the tax implications and the higher tax bracket on all your income or what the extra hours and responsibilities may mean, losing precious time with your loved ones or bedtime with your children. A person is also ineligible for a GST cheque when they reach a certain amount of income, yet they still pay the GST. Like myself, once I got married I lost all tax benefits (GST rebate and my child tax benefit was cut in half). So what do people actually make and spend money on?

Simple Summary of Cost of Living in Canada

Family of four estimated monthly costs: C$5,372.
Single person estimated monthly costs: C$2,924.

Cost of living in Canada is more expensive than in 70% of countries in the World (26 out of 84). They say there is no longer a middle class in Canada.[6]

This summary is based on 900 square foot living, and a new Volkswagen vehicle worth $25,000. Is this even real-

---

6   "Cost of Living in Canada," Expatistan (website), accessed July 14, 2020, https://www.expatistan.com/cost-of-living/country/canada

istic? With the housing crisis and growing families, in most cases neither of these would be practical.

A full-time minimum wage worker makes almost $600 less than the single person estimated monthly cost and that is prior to income tax. The median after-tax income of Canadian families and unattached individuals was $61,400 in 2018, virtually unchanged from 2017. This is less income than the estimated family cost of living listed above. I feel in Canada, it is very easy for a person to live beyond their means because the cost of living is rapidly increasing, such as (house and car) insurance, which saw up to an 11% increase in 2020.[7]

Based on these numbers, there isn't room for a family to save for college or emergencies. I've experienced it myself, credit card debt increasing slightly, but it's not within means to pay it. It compounds. Your child will need a student loan, so you will be starting them off in adulthood from a place of debt. Your car breaks down and you can't fix it, so the easy approval on a new financed vehicle that you can't *actually* afford, is the *right now* solution—leaving you with years of interest payments and at a depreciation rate that makes this not a sound investment. And in my case, that thing that shook my entire future was a costly legal battle my ex forced upon me.

When I was battling him through Provincial Family Court, I began to realize even more what a struggle it is to be a middle class woman in Canada. Because of mine and

7   "Auto Insurance Rates in Ontario Going Up As Much As 11%," CBC News (website), with files from Nick Boisvert, last updated February 10, 2020, https://www.google.ca/amp/s/www.cbc.ca/amp/1.5458360

my spouse's combined salaries, I was ineligible for support from the government; legal aid and housing support, to name a few—so I could continue to tread strongly toward my end goal, relocating my family for a better, more affordable life in Ontario. Instead, pairing our day-to-day financial woes with a family court battle not initiated by us, meant bye-bye to any extras and hello to researching how the hell we were going to stay afloat.

Navigating the Provincial Court system can be tricky, but it is structured in such a way that one should be able to help themselves without hiring a costly lawyer. The issue though, the court system does not follow their own law or guidelines, I am speaking specifically to their timelines laid out clearly on their forms: 30 days, 60 days, must complete this form, that form, etc. Leniency is given, or so I have been told by a handful of lawyers, to those without a lawyer or to the ones who seem to be at a disadvantage. In my case, my ex utilized his difficulty reading and processing information to drag me through court, pointing out that he did not understand the guidelines of the paperwork. The lack of communication between him and I when issues or changes in his life arose was a huge downfall. The court trial and multiple appearances could have been avoided if the courts followed their own guidelines and put us into mediation or with a counsellor after our first appearance.[8] I asked repeatedly for this, but was always made out to be the controlling ex, and instead they went in his favour

---

8   "Get a Final Family Order in Provincial Court If You Can't Both Agree," Family Law (website), accessed July 14, 2020, https://familylaw.lss.bc.ca/bc-legal-system/court-orders/get-order-bc/provincial-court/get-final-family-order-provincial-0#4

by proceeding with a trial. Mediation had worked for us once, and I agreed to doing it again at his request to sort out our issues, but instead my ex changed his mind and filed application after application and got us in front of a judge. In reality, our case should've been opened and shut right away because my ex missed his deadline to file and there should've been consequences for that, according to the Family Law Act (Division 6, 68).[9] For a brief snippet of how I got into this court mess, as mentioned before the goal was to relocate my family from British Columbia to Ontario with our child. My ex had been in and out of our daughters life for a couple of years and, at the point of giving him written notice of my intent to relocate, he had not seen her in close to seven months and spoke to her on a very on again, off again schedule. Based on the requirements through the Family Law Act, he then had 30 days from me notifying him to file an application to object to the move—he waited seventy-six days to file his application to prohibit the move.

Regardless of this blatant disregard for the court process, he moved close to my town without notice and quit his job of many years where he made close to double what I did at the time, only to end up unemployed and then on minimum wage, living for free with a distant relative, to try to lower what the judge would require him to pay in child support. Financially, what he did made sense for him, morally and ethically (in my opinion) it did not. With-

---

9   "Family Law Act," Gov.bc.ca (website), last updated June 24, 2020, http://www.bclaws.ca/civix/document/id/complete/statreg/11025_04#section66

in weeks our court journey began and continued on for twelve months. He also originally got into court by filing the wrong document; there are specific steps to follow, or so I thought, for getting in front of a judge; he lied on his affidavits, changed information on each application, and his lawyer skipped all guidelines, rules, and requirements, yet he got in anyways. One court clerk even asked how his lawyer had gotten so far off the wrong document. I tried to get the judge to recognize that this is classified as court harassment,[10] but was brushed aside.

Being served multiple forms by my ex within a period of seven days had me in a panic, I did everything I could to try to get quick legal help. Hiring a lawyer was my last option—they make 10 times per hour what I do, so how can a person afford this?—and I was at a loss and feeling the pressure. Legal aid[11] in BC wasn't able to help me because I made too much money, even though the cost of living in Canada is $5,372 and their threshold for a family of four is $3,650 net income per month. Well my spouse and I at the time made more than that, but due to the cost of living we were simply getting by without thousands in savings to pay a law firm. Even though my daughter that I was fighting for in court was not biologically his, my husband's income was still taken into account. Then there

---

10   "If Your Spouse is Harassing You Through the Courts," Family Law (website), accessed July 14, 2020, https://familylaw.lss.bc.ca/abuse-family-violence/it-abuse/if-your-spouse-harassing-you-through-courts

11   "Do I Qualify for Legal Representations?" Legal Aid BC (website), accessed July 14, 2020, https://lss.bc.ca/legal_aid/doIQualifyRepresentation

was the option of Aboriginal Legal Aid[12] in BC, which has the same financial guidelines, the only difference was the option of financial assistance (welfare),[13] which again my family made too much money to utilize and my family's Indigenous status was taken from us decades ago, so I didn't qualify anyway.

I have prided myself on being a hard-working woman and mother, but I felt let down, almost like I would've been better off (to qualify for subsidized or free, urgent legal help) to be unemployed, so I could receive the help I needed from the system. But that is not me.

Every phone call, email, briefing, paper printed, and appearance at the courthouse cost me legal fees. Our retainer ($5,000) was gone in less than a week because of all the documents my ex served me with; it was a "fluster fuck" (as one Duty Counsel lawyer called my case) to sort through. I was told this is a legal tactic used to drown a person in paperwork so they can no longer afford legal help. In family law, the motive is supposed to be "the best interest of the child"—I don't see how this behaviour favoured my daughter in any way. I am an organized person, especially when it comes to paperwork, and I had a hard time wrapping my head around all of the documentation. The increasing bill and the pending trial and preparations were amounting to tens of thousands of dollars. This bill

12   "Legal Aid for Aboriginal People in BC," Aboriginal Legal Aid in BC (website), accessed July 14, 2020, https://aboriginal.legalaid.bc.ca/

13   Penny Goldsmith, "How to Apply for Welfare," *Legal Services Society BC*, first edition (March 2017), https://pubsdb.lss.bc.ca/pdfs/pubs/How-to-Apply-for-Welfare-eng.pdf

puts any middle class family into poverty for that year because any loan obtained will collect a minimum of thousands of dollars in interest. It's a cycle that can't not be paid off without doubling a salary.

I did my best with what I had and I utilized Duty Counsel[14] at the courthouse, but there is only so much they can help with when you have maybe ten minutes to give them the spiel on your whole case (my case file was probably 200 pages by this point). Duty Counsel usually meant a different lawyer each time, who was dealing with upwards of twenty cases a day, so their brain capacity to get you what you need cannot be counted on. I have received incorrect advice from two out of the three lawyers I spoke to, which got me turned around in the court proceedings. These mix ups led to our one-day hearing regarding relocating with my daughter turning into a seven day trial and multiple other court appearances that spanned nine months. Since I did not qualify for legal aid, I turned to the Justice Access Centre to take advantage of the few free appointments I could get.

I ended up taking out a last minute, high interest loan to pay a portion of my legal fees and when that got burnt up, I had to borrow an additional $15,000 from family members with no pay back arrangements possible in the near future. But thankfully my family believed enough in my case that they would do anything to assist. With these new financial pressures I also looked into rental housing

14   "Duty Counsel Lawyers for Family Law Matters," Legal Aid BC (website), accessed July 14, 2020, https://legalaid.bc.ca/legal_aid/familyDutyCounsel

assistance.[15] Surprise, surprise, I did not qualify as their household threshold is $35,000 per year. Being married, I did not qualify because of my spouse's income. Again I thought, *I should just quit everything and have the government pay my way.* But that is not me! The juggling act continued as I trudged forward through the muck that was this court battle.

For years I struggled to have my daughter's father in her life. I would over accommodate—constantly monitoring my phone and emails, waiting to bend at his every demand with only a day or two notice of him wanting to see her. My family wondered why I was so lenient toward his expectations for her to be available when it was convenient for him, they asked why I didn't just say no or put my foot down. Well, in Canada it is very common that the raising of children after separation often falls on the woman, and if it looked (even slightly) like I was denying him parenting time, or if I showed any weakness to him regarding our daughter, I knew there would be a knock at my door with another court application. I lived in constant angst, and still do, waiting for the next document to drop at my door, for the next large manila envelope to come in the mail, or for the next email, phone call, or last minute visit. So when months passed without him calling or seeing her (for the third time), with him not supporting her financially throughout her life, and with no co-parenting support from him, it came time for me to wake up to the

---

15   "Rental Assistance Program (RAP)," BC Housing (website), accessed July 14, 2020, https://www.bchousing.org/housing-assistance/rental-assistance/RAP

fact that her future was only up to me. I often wondered if it were me, the mother, that was the neglectful one, would that be as accepted as a neglectful father? Would I have had as much power as he did in the courtroom? Would a lawyer pull the "family gatekeeper"[16] card in court if our caretaker roles were reversed? We followed the court rules, gave proper written notice, we let the mandatory time, communicated with the father's side of the family, packed our bags, accepted job offers in Ontario, sought out housing, and were set to move. Although we followed the rules, and he didn't, we had to pause our move and stay in BC, which we could not afford, and hire a legal team. Incurring an extra $32,000 plus in rent, groceries, and hydro alone and $40,000 plus in legal, this is well over a years income, which will take me years to settle. Our future for my daughter was on fire and he was dumping gas all over it. In the end, the truth prevailed and we "won"—if you can call any of this "winning." Now the relationship with him is more of a struggle because of the anguish he put us all through, including his daughter.

With mountains of debt, and the credit score I worked so hard on bettering prior to the original intent to move dwindled, I was flat out broke; fighting for my daughter's rights against a system that is supposed to have her best interest at heart, in mind, and at the forefront. What we lost was years of her childhood and a down payment on a family house in Ontario, where real estate and cost of

16   Robert Farzad, "Are Child Custody Laws That Treat Parental Gatekeeping like Child Abuse Long Overdue?" Huffpost (blog), last updated October 12, 2014, https://www.huffpost.com/entry/are-specific-child-custody-gate-keeping_b_5666848

living is manageable, and in Eastern Ontario, the job opportunities are plentiful.

I can say that pushing forward was the most stressful time of my life, but I accept it as a learning experience and a success; although I dug myself into a deeper hole financially, and my marriage became strained and unraveled, I have begun to see the light at the end of the tunnel. The juggling act continues and I tread daily through the waters that I have laid out as my life; I am working to conquer my debt and my past, to work forward and provide for my family, and to learn about and embrace my heritage in the process. If it weren't for my oldest sister and her savvy investments, my middle sister and her constant emotional support, my mother and her guidance with my children, and my few close friends who have provided immense support through this whole process of *adulthood*, I would not be where I am today. I'd likely still be stuck in a toxic relationship with my ex and still living paycheque-to-paycheque. So now I am free and I have a bright future ahead of me, and my daughters; I will pave the way for them and show them what a confident, mixed raced woman in business and relationships looks like. I am strong, newly outspoken and opinionated, and embracing it all—the good, the bad, the crazy, and the ugly. It is easy to *look* successful and happy, but I want to be the me I know I can be; successful in business, healthy, and genuinely happy. So I strive now to provide a safe household for my girls, to be financially stable in our crazy economy, and wish to have knowledge about who we are—all heritage included—to share with my daughters.

STEPH CLARK

French Canadian | Jamaican | Ska Nah Doht First Nations
ig: @stephkmua

Beautiful brown, golden honey skin, big brown
    eyes, and kinky hair is not beauty in your
    eyes. I am beautiful.
My skin tone should not be the measurement of
    my worth.
It should not dictate where I am allowed to go,
    who I am allowed to be, after all we live in
    the land of the free.
Our fathers and mothers, fathers and mothers
    were put down, held down and chained and
    their voices screamed for change.
Yet we can't seem to maintain,
a system that gives us a voice, a way to be equal,
    is this just the sequel to the past?
A way to keep our people from rising and shin-
    ing, how long will this last?
No longer will you hold us down, our voices
    have been found and we will fight for our
    rights, and be heard, be seen.

You can't hold us down any longer.

We have united as one, our battles will be won, our freedom will be sung.

How many Elijah's, Breonna's, George's, Eric's, Tamir's will it take before our people do not have to live in fear?

No longer will mothers have to shed a thousand tears for their children taken in an instance, our voices will be heard.

Chapter Eight

LIFE IS NOT TRULY DEFINED WITHOUT FREEDOM

*"Internal personal power
and character is born through
the resiliency and strength
you exhibit when faced with
conflict and adversity."*

NADIA DEDIC

Nadia Dedic

Canadian and Czech citizen

www.dedicatedliving.com

ig: nd_squared | fb: Dedicated Living

Photographer: Dennis Duong
ig: @motiondphotography @motiond_headshots
www.motionphotography.com

Nadia is a Certified Raw Foods Chef (CRFC) with the Raw Food Chef Alliance. She attended the Pachavega vegan culinary school specializing in raw food chef training and plant-based culinary arts. This led her on a distinct path to learning more about health and vitality and implementing a positive philosophy of living life through the integration of a healthy diet and lifestyle. Nadia is currently enrolled in the Precision Nutrition Level 1 Program, which is home to some of the world's top nutrition coaches. With this training she hopes to continue to share her life experiences and knowledge to help motivate and empower others to live a healthy and vibrant life.

Nadia obtained her Viking Ninja's Mindfulness Mechanics and Steel Mace Yoga Level 1 certification through Erik Melland and Erin Furry, the Onnit Gym Steel Mace Master Coach and trainer to UFC Champions. Nadia also has her Paddle into Fitness Stand-up Paddle (SUP), SUP Yoga and SUP Fitness Certifications and received her Level 1 WPA (World Paddle Association) Certificate in 2019. Nadia is a believer in the power of the mind and its ability to exceed perceived limits and hopes to empower others in their own journey to health and wellness. She is also a contributing author to best-selling book *Fitness to Freedom* published by Golden Brick Road Publishing House.

I've always been inspired by the cultural fabric of this country; its spirit of identity, generosity of vision, and the strength of its inclusion. Factors that drive Canada's legacy of diversity and rich cultural history.

My father emigrated to Canada from Czechoslovakia (the Czech Republic) at a time when it was under a totalitarian regime. He was a young man in search of freedom and a purpose for life. As poignantly phrased by Albert Einstein, *"everything that is really great and inspiring is created by the individual who can labor in freedom."*

As a child, I had no concept of immigration, cultural diversity, or what life is like growing up in another country. My father left his homeland, on his own with no support or family. No money. No security. No knowledge of the English language. Only the courage and dream of a better future.

I was born in London, Ontario and grew up and spent my childhood in Kincardine, Ontario. A small municipality situated on Lake Huron that had a population at the time of less than 1700 people. Raised in a small community, cultural diversity was not as prevalent as it was in larger cities across Canada.

The community in which I was raised had no other Czech citizens. As my mother was Canadian, I never learned to speak Czech. My father's family remained in the Czech Republic and was not around to instill the fundamental cultural traditions of my father's homeland or speak to the diversity of my family history.

My father, a quiet and humble man, never spoke of his experiences or hardships growing up. His coping mechanism was to suppress any negative experiences and not speak of the pain or trauma. Dissociation is something we all do and it is a vital part of our ingrained survival system.[1] My father's inability to speak of his past was an adaptive defence mechanism established to disconnect from the trauma to which he was exposed. He chose instead to focus on a future of possibilities and opportunities. It was not until I became an adult that I discovered the magnitude of struggles that my father endured to ensure a greater life for his family.

He lived in a refugee camp for six months in Europe until he received sponsorship to come initially to Montreal, Canada. He did not have any knowledge of the English language, so that created a significant barrier. Also, issues regarding access to housing, local services, and employment opportunities were more limited, particularly back then in the late 1960s early 1970s. Although my father was Eastern European, he faced prejudice and discrimination regarding his lack of the English language, and when he was able to secure employment and improved language skills, he faced many challenges communicating with an accent that often left him excluded from others. He was

---

1   https://www.goodtherapy.org/blog/the-brain-in-defense-mode-how-dissociation-helps-us-survive-0429155; April 29, 2015 • By Anastasia Pollock, LCMHC

isolated during his initial transition to the country and it took time to build a network of friends and support.

He recalls, *"I got scheduled for English as a second language program for five or six months, and an arrangement for room and board. As a single person I did qualify for $20.00 weekly allowance from which I had to pay the cost of room and board $12.00 weekly, public transportation cost to and from the school. With the rest of my weekly allowance, which was about $3.00 I could do as I like. My first money that I did earn was placing inserts in commercial flyers in the newspaper. My first $10.00. After, followed a couple of low paying jobs. It was clear that sound knowledge of the English language was a gateway for better paid employment opportunities and became an extreme priority. When you land your first well paid job everything changes. You will start dreaming and making these dreams a reality. Canada is a land of dreams. You have a dream, make it a reality and have another dream."*

There are no words to describe what I saw in his heart in that moment. The pride of how far he had come, the hard work he endured that paid off immeasurably, and the realization that he ultimately accomplished what he set out to do; provide his children with a better place to live with greater opportunity.

Living in a multicultural society, as the daughter of an immigrant father, I became increasingly curious about my heritage as I got older. This curiosity led me to believe that in order to truly know one's self, you need to study and understand your family lineage and history. Your ethnic background is an integral and fundamental part of your identity. The more I was able to acquire knowledge about my heritage, I unexpectedly began to understand myself in a more profound way. Knowing where you come from provides crucial insight into figuring out where you're going.

In Canadian society, it is hard to learn about different heritages, lineage, and history. Particularly when you don't have extended family from your home country to instill first-hand knowledge. You really have to make the effort and time to research, speak with others from the same cultural backgrounds, speak to your parents about their experiences and educate yourself. Becoming involved in a Czech community where you live, if available, or any other ethic background that may apply to you, will offer community support. This is instrumental in connecting you to others with similar cultural traditions who are generally willing to offer support and guidance when needed.

LIFE IN A TIME OF TURMOIL

"This is no time for ease and comfort. It is time to dare and ensure" -Winston Churchill

My father defines an extraordinary life as the freedom of time, place, and company. A simple yet powerful statement. Freedom is not something tangible that you can grasp, articulate into words, or adequately describe once acquired. It's not a title or prestige. It is most valued by those who've had it taken away.

My father was born and raised in Czechoslovakia during an era where the political scene in the country was complex, to say the least. After World War II, the country's national economy spiraled out of control and a communist-dominated government began to organize. Czechoslovakia, once a democratic country, became a communist state whose political decisions were largely dictated by the Soviet Union.[2]

As the daughter of an immigrant, born and raised in Canada, I found it difficult to comprehend or relate to the socioeconomic or psychological impact that results from losing one's own liberties and way of life. The complete restriction to freedom of choice and action. The gradual degradation of a moral society. Corruption. Destitution. Loss of personal identity. Fear of condemnation. Living under a regime that denies you of your basic human rights becomes about a daily struggle for survival.

Admittedly, I was naïvely ignorant at the time. Never having been exposed to oppression, the concept in my mind was abstract. When you're born in a country where you've only ever known the freedoms and responsibilities of being a Canadian, you don't know any other way of life. My understanding of the concept of communism or life in an oppressive, war-torn country, was derived mainly from media coverage of global events. As well as any literature I read on the topic. Both of which rarely captured the realities.

The frequency of hearing about global tragedies of other citizens, and the helplessness you feel towards certain injustices, has a subtle way of desensitizing you. I

---

2   Tracy Burns, "Communism in Czechoslovakia," Private Prague Guide (website), accessed July 14, 2020, https://www.private-prague-guide.com/article/communism-in-czechoslovakia/

found myself, whether consciously or unconsciously, disassociating. It was simply a concept in my mind. As I was not able to touch it, smell it, or experience it, the realization unfolded that unless you've lived it first-hand, it can never be truly understood. *"It is one thing to study war and another to live a warrior's life."* -Steven Pressfield, *The War of Art.*

I've always had the privilege of enjoying the freedoms and responsibilities that come with Canadian citizenship. You become acclimatized and take for granted the things in life of which you have always known or experienced.

At eighteen, I was starting my first year at university and was working at one of the top five national banks as a bank teller. I lived on my own with the support of my parents. I was independent. I had the freedom to go to school, to choose where to live, how to spend my time, who to associate with, and spent my money as I saw fit. I did so with a discerning sense of comfort and confidence.

By contrast at eighteen, my father was living at the mercy of a government that took pride in persecuting and restricting the rights of its own people. In his own words he described the following:

> *"The key to survival in this country was work. Since ever I can remember you do something all the time. Work, work, work. It is embedded in you. Everyone must work. That is your strength and your wealth.*
> *You get up early in the morning, 4:30 or 5:00, hustle to your workplace, and go home at 15:00. During the day any free time that you*

have is used up by thinking; what will you eat in the morning, lunch, dinner today, tomorrow, on the weekend? Can you afford to buy what you plan to have? Is this the best you can do? How long will you have to stand in line at the general groceries store, the butcher, fruit and vegetable stores to purchase what you will need? Do you have time to make it? Will you need fridge access to keep it fresh?

How can you think about anything else if you spend so much of your mental capacity on necessities as meals? The rationing of water, showering time, electricity, and the high prices for gasoline became accepted as the norm.

Sooner or later you learn that you cannot live on the idea alone. What do you do? You have no hope. You have no future. You have lost confidence in yourself. In the old country you have no financial opportunities and your successes are measured by one opportunity that may happen once in your life. Buying a car or flat to live in; Going on a memorable vacation or having a hobby of sorts. That is all you can do. You live in a place that scares you so much that you feel as though there are no choices for you. You fear for your life. You get depressed. Your mind is left to wander and explore any options to escape. One of the last choices you have, if you're lucky, is to escape."

You can't ever imagine or prepare yourself for this to happen in life. "*A low-grade misery begins to pervade everything.*" -Steven Pressfield, *The War of Art*. And when it does, I imagine you find yourself questioning, is this all there is that life has to offer me? What do I do? How do I act? Is there anything else out there for me?

At a time in which you are faced with a situation, that of which you cannot control, and your basic rights are stripped away, sorrow replaces joy in your life.

> "*I spent an hour with laughter; we chatted all the way. But I barely remember a single thing from what she had to say. I then spent an hour with sorrow; and nearly a word said she. But oh the things I learned that day that sorrow walked with me.*" -Robert Browning

It is the most difficult of times and moments of adversity that end up defining our strength of character. As Anna Yusim succinctly noted "*these moments carry credibility precisely because they are not anticipated or prescribed. They are, however, transformative.*"

We all have a breaking point. The reality is that extreme hardships, the unraveling of different facets of your life, and multi-systemic injustices inevitably happen. If you grant them power, it can pervade and corrupt every aspect of your life, or conversely serve as a catalyst to drive impactful change.

"Most of us have two lives. The life that we live, and the unlived life within us. Between the two stands Resistance." -Steven Pressfield, *The War of Art*

No one chooses to become a refugee. No one chooses to leave anyone behind, including those they love, their prized possessions, or childhood memories. Most importantly, no one chooses to leave their homeland and the familiarity of the only place they've known.

Yet as history dictates, every hero's journey begins with a crisis or call to action.

I imagine how many times my father, consciously or subconsciously, reflects on the past. The idea of a young man forced to leave his home and loved ones to pursue a better future is unfathomable to me. I try to imagine the magnitude of feelings that he must have experienced during that time frame; guilt, fear, shame, desperation, and angst. Memories and emotions so impactful, that may face with passage of time, but never disappear.

My father further elaborates on his experience and shares his written thoughts:

> *"During that time, communists made it clear that they are here to stay and there is nothing you can do about it. You will do what they tell you and if you do not, you are an enemy of the state. Political correctness became a way of life. What happened to democracy?*
> *Any questions that could remotely introduce a thought or a hesitation in omnipresence of*

communist party were dealt with swiftly and with extreme prejudice. Any religion was considered competition to the ideal communist idea. Humans were no longer viewed as people, but as mere commodities. If you were born into this unfortunate era it is difficult to know the difference. You are consistently brainwashed and led to believe that this is the ideal life, the life you will live."

What I find most compelling about his story, is that it provides insight into how to overcome fear and discomfort. His belief was that if he could endure these temporary hardships, then a life of freedom, justice, and liberty awaited him. The mindset that hope will prevail. *"In the midst of every crisis, lies great opportunity."* -Albert Einstein.

In his decision to escape communism, all he knew was the unknown. The inner conflict, isolation, and desperation that he must have experienced and endured can not be articulated into words. The constant self-doubt. The incessant questioning of whether you are making the right decision, and if so, at what cost? When freedom is at stake, there are no costs you wouldn't bear. As Herbert Douglas describes, *"the cost of freedom is incalculable."*

In troubled times you learn to consistently make choices that stand for love, compassion, courage, sustainability, and possibility. You adopt these strategies until they become part of your identity. The sense of hope that comes with moving to a new country that is known for liberty and justice, provides a crucial level of comfort.

"We understand that we want to be better but have no clear definition of what better means and that is part of the process."

-Madison Taylor

Statistics alone are not able to tell the fundamental stories of immigration. People's first hand experiences do. Since its inception, this nation has been continually infused with the energy of newcomers. Yet their assimilation has seldom been smooth.[3]

As noted by my father:

"If you go through the process of emigration when you are very young and alone, you find yourself exposed to a number of different elements imposed by the surrounding society. You will be tested, and you may falter. You must remember this is not the end of you, or your world. It is a fresh new start and you give it all you have again because you are a dreamer.

Have as much fun as you can handle, go fishing, pick up a cause. I did have some dreams of my own. I wanted to be free and live as a free man. I wanted to have my family and my family to live as free citizens all their lives. I am happy that is exactly what did happen. I strive to be part of this country as a Canadian citizen, not just as some place to stay but the place I call my home."

---

3   "Share Your Story," My Immigration Story (website), accessed July 14, 2020, https://myimmigrationstory.com/

In his internal uprising, my father found the courage to free himself. He was compelled by his own internal revolution. When you become conscious of your own power you find resiliency, flexibility, and strength beyond imagination. Pushing the boundaries of what you believe to be possible often leads to limitless empowerment.

> *"No problem is permanent, and nothing that happens is pervasive."* -Tony Robbins

Born and raised as a Canadian citizen, I was not exposed to the racism and exclusion that my father endured as an immigrant in a new country. An invaluable lesson born through my dad's story was to never take for granted those liberties of which you are afforded. His stories remind me that not everything in life will work easily, that disappointments occur and inequalities exist, but that we can recover, triumph, and find happiness despite hardships.

Life moves at an extraordinary pace. We need to learn to be able to slow down and appreciate and be grateful for everything we have. We are constantly preoccupied with the things we don't have or experiences we are missing out on; yet we are more fortunate than so many other individuals. If we all stopped for a moment and examined what was available to us, we would find endless possibilities. No dream is too big.

My father taught me to treat others with compassion and make the most of what life has to offer. Being aware of and suspending any judgemental behaviour had been instilled in me at a young age. There is no value in discriminating or judging others based on their names, the colour of their skin, or in the way they speak or dress. If you are going to judge someone make sure it is based on solid facts of the situation and the person, and how you are directly being treated by that individual. Any judgements of others should not lead to generalizations of different countries or cultures or people.

Live a humble but impactful life, believe in your own self-worth, and don't ever allow anyone to tell you that you or an idea that you have, is not worthy. Do not allow anyone to discourage you. Make sure you have a very solid foundation of self-esteem that will allow you to excel in life, despite other's perceptions or discriminations against you. Reach out to family and friends when you are in need and always go back to the concept that we are all unique and have something to offer. I find when I am discouraged, misjudged, misunderstood, or undervalued based on my sex, race or appearance, the one thing that brings me joy and validation is connecting to others and offering help and support without any expectation of something in return.

We live in an unprecedented time where we are faced with challenges on many different fronts. Yet, we have the ability to rise above it, to exert our powers though advocacy and educating others. As we navigate this uncertain period, we are presented with the opportunity to be introspective and reflect on what is inherently important to us—family and community. What we may have taken for granted in the past, we are now armed with the power to acknowledge and honor the hardships endured by our immigrant parents. Let us ensure that their courageous efforts are recognized and passed on through our own generation.

Don't let your voice go unheard and don't let another opportunity pass you by, because together we can bring remarkable and lasting change to this world. If we take the time to learn from our parents' experiences, share these stories and show our vulnerabilities, we can create breakthroughs and awaken the human spirit in everyone.

No matter where we come from or what we believe in, when we accept our differences and bring humanity together, we grow together as a nation. Let's advance the capacity of our collective future by sharing our stories, owning our history and cultural backgrounds, and helping develop a community of support and acceptance.

Chapter Nine

THE GYM SHOES

"With love and kindness we can come together as a nation and celebrate the great diversity of humankind ensuring equal opportunities and freedoms for all Canadians."

ANGEL KIBBLE CPL (RET'D)

Angel Kibble

Dutch | Scottish

www.AngelEmpowerment.ca

ig: @AngelEmpowerment | fb: @AngelEmpowerment
p: @AngelEmpowerment
Goodreads: Angel Empowerment

Angel Kibble is a mother, author, and Canadian Army Veteran who draws on her life's story, intuition, and passion to inspire, empower, and encourage others to embrace a healthy, fulfilling, and purpose driven life. Angel is a new rising author and Trauma Informed Certified Coach. She embraces a holistic approach to the challenges of life while maintaining a slower pace and allowing a healthy balance in life while nurturing her soul. Born in Sarnia, Ontario, and spending most of her youth in the Okanagan, Angel now resides with her husband, children, and her service dog on beautiful Vancouver Island. Her journey through life, though not as she envisioned, is one of hope, inspiration, and true resilience. Being the warrior she is, Angel will continue to share stories from her soul in future publications including an upcoming book series.

Patiently waiting, handsome as ever in his tuxedo, he stood in the partial shaded relief of a large gnarled *Arbutus* tree. Taking care not to snag my dress, I gingerly exited the passenger seat with the assistance of a dear friend who had driven me in his pickup to this magical sunlit bay. An occasional breeze whispered her way up the cliffs from the water offering minimal relief from the blistering hot sun. Immediately my eyes locked onto Daddy's normally stoic grey-blue eyes; glistening with the misty pools of tears that built in the corners, his wrinkled wise eyes locked onto mine with unconditional love and pride. Without a word, we embraced, sharing more than any words could at that moment.

Arm in arm we approached the steep steps. I paused, so I could take it all in, ground myself with a few deep breaths, and let go of the chaos of the day leading up to that moment. I carefully started calculating how we would navigate our way down the steep steps to the carpeted ramp, onto the dock, and finally up onto the ship as we had practiced the evening prior. Daddy held me a little closer and whispered, "You are truly beautiful, I've got you . . . I'll be here holding you up every step of the way." Standing in my beautiful sparkling high heels, my left leg shook uncontrollably from instability and a lack of strength. My leg felt like it was on fire from the uncontrollable pain of Complex Regional Pain Syndrome, the result of a military training injury years earlier. After two years between a wheelchair and crutches, I was now determined as ever. I mentally walked myself through the ceremony one more time as my eyes naturally flowed over the steps to the red carpeted ramp, the crowded dock, and the narrow aisle between the seats. I lovingly scanned the rows of guests, exposed to the hot sun and sitting patiently in perfectly aligned white chairs while the brass from the quintet sparkled in the sunlight as their rich music filled the bay. My gaze then rested on the love of my life, handsome as ever, standing tall and proud in his high collar whites, sword resting at his hip and glistening as the sun reflecting from the ornate gold hilt. He was waiting patiently aboard the ninety-two-year-old, one hundred and two foot long sailing ship, which was elegantly berthed alongside the freshly cleaned and decorated dock. The guests were anxiously awaiting my long overdue arrival. My gaze settled on the beautiful blue water beyond the ship to the very spot where I fell in love with the ocean and with Jeff, the man I was about to marry. Arms locked and a smile on my face, I washed away the thoughts of all the obstacles I had overcome, the sacrifices I and so many others made long ago that gave me the freedom I enjoyed today. I was finally ready. Filled with a calm determination, I mustered all my strength and locked onto Daddy's arm with complete trust and faith as we stepped out for all to see.

A few years prior, the day had finally come for Jeff and I to venture out on my first sailing trip. I was always captivated with Jeff's excitement and passion as he told stories of growing up sailing the Gulf Islands with his grandfather, an avid sailor. His words made it quite apparent this was a lifestyle for him rather than a sport. I could feel a nervous excitement creep over me as we chatted and unloaded our weekend necessities into a handy wheelbarrow that seemed to be eagerly awaiting our arrival at the top of the dock. Maneuvering the wheelbarrow and a few other items in tow, we arrived at our newly purchased twenty-eight foot sailboat. April Sun was old and weathered, but we proudly gazed at her resting in her berth. Extending his arm and firmly taking my hand, he helped me climb aboard. You could almost hear the excitement that was silently stirring in him finally having the opportunity to introduce me to this part of his world. At the same time I could feel excitement within myself as I anticipated a week of *gunkholing*, a West Coast boating term for meandering from place to place and staying overnight in random bays. We secured our items and scrubbed the bottom of the boat from the foredeck as the clunky old one-cylinder diesel engine loudly rumbled and shook like an antique farm tractor as she warmed up. Without a word and after a quiet gentle kiss we silently agreed it was time to slip from the dock.

There was no time like the present to be thrown in feet first. As Jeff let slip the lines, he challenged me to drive the boat out of the harbour. A calm anxiousness swept through me as I mentally talked myself through the departure. Like a natural, I carefully maneuvered away from the docks, past neighbouring sailboats, and around nearby rocks. Soon I was navigating through the harbour towards Fisgard Lighthouse noting how different the navy dockyard looked from the water. As we passed by the building where I had first met Jeff, I listened to his calm experienced voice; something he had developed through his years as a Royal Canadian Navy Navigation Officer. This brought me great comfort, as I am sure it did with his many navigation students prior. Each new directive came with an explanation. I greatly appreciated his constructive instruction style.

Westward bound and with our zodiac in tow, we motored at full throttle; a mere four knots was all that April Sun could manage! With just a few hours until sunset, we decided to pull into a beautiful little bay tucked in behind Albert Head. My next lesson was lowering the anchor, which went smoothly as we waved at nearby friends who coincidentally chose the same bay to anchor their boat for the night. The smell of our charcoal barbecue lingered in the night sky as we prepared, cooked, and ate a delicious steak dinner. I went down below to tidy up when Jeff suddenly, but quietly, urged me to come back to the cockpit. Unsure why, I quickly slipped back up and found myself speechless and in awe as I stared at the most beautiful creature I had ever seen! Just fifteen feet from our boat was a massive transient killer whale gently swimming on the surface circling our boat. Jeff held me close as we listened and watched as the whale gently dove and surfaced, breathing loudly from his blowhole every few minutes as he hunted salmon. It was mesmerizing and surreal as I realized that only a few millimetres of fibreglass stood between us and the beautiful, yet rather large hungry mammal. A few minutes later he was gone.

The picturesque evening, almost like our own fairy tale, found us under the most amazing blanket of stars sipping a full-bodied blended red as we talked about our past histories and future dreams. I explained the challenges and extreme adversity I had endured through my formative years, which included not knowing my biological origin. Having never known my father, I naturally embraced my stepfather. I adopted his rich Dutch heritage as my own. Captivated by all I was sharing as we got to know each other, Jeff urged me to continue sharing my family history.

Trying to keep my thoughts organized despite having so many to share, I continued. Opa and Oma, who I sadly never had the opportunity to meet, had lived a humble life raising eight children leading up to and throughout WWII in the Netherlands. They operated a small bridge along a canal in exchange for a small stipend and use of a quaint brick house in the countryside near Groningen city. When Nazi Germany conquered their way across Europe, Opa was taken prisoner along with countless other men mandated to work in a Nazi labour camp—leaving Oma and thousands of other families praying for the safe return of their husbands, fathers, and sons. Oma did her best to keep life as *normal* as she could during the occupation, watching over her young family and manning the bridge, which kept them housed and fed. Opa was returned a few months later bringing great relief to Oma and their young family though he was never the same. His young children, my dad included, were blissfully unaware and too young to understand how close they were to losing their father.

Pausing to ground myself, I apologised as I took a few deep breaths to calm my quivering voice. I found it stressful to imagine the hardship and fear my family must have endured so many years ago. Listening to the gentle sound of the water lapping at the boat's hull and feeling the soothing roll of our boat like a mother lovingly comforting her child, the tightness in my chest and invisible lump in my throat soon eased. I continued.

As Nazi soldiers poured into the Netherlands and the local government replaced with the tyranny of a Gestapo headquarters, backed up by cruel Nazi SS soldiers, Oma and Opa did their best to shelter their children from the terror, starvation, and danger all around them. Daddy, his siblings, and the neighbouring children would run, swim, and play; and although they were cautious and kept their distance, soldiers would regularly come and go from their small home as they pleased. Despite Nazi directives banning radios, Oma and Opa hid their tiny black one inside an old piano that had been converted into a linen storage space. Evenings found them secretly huddled around the tiny black box listening to the Dutch Underground Resistance broadcasts. One night SS soldiers stormed their little brick house seizing the radio, arresting Opa, and disappearing with him into the night. Desperate, Oma acted quickly knowing Opa would never return if she didn't take immediate action. With a bottle of wine she had hidden away, she rushed to the neighbours pleading for any assistance they could spare. The neighbour handed her a hundred guilders, worth several thousand dollars today, which she tucked safely in her pocket and rushed by bicycle ten kilometres to the city of Groningen. The Gestapo had set up their headquarters after commandeering *Scholtenhuis*, a large private residence of a wealthy businessman in the heart of Groningen city. Many people were tortured and executed there as the Gestapo tried to dismantle the Dutch Resistance and exert local control. Terrified and without options, Oma gave a short prayer hoping she wasn't too late before she marched up to the SS soldier guarding the exterior door of Scholtenhuis. Desperate yet poised, she was able to negotiate her husband's freedom in exchange for the wine and the borrowed money by taking advantage of the guard's greed. Opa was soon led from the basement holding area and tossed to the street. Relieved and terrified, Oma and Opa safely made their way back home.

"I can't even begin to imagine," I tearfully whispered. Jeff mentioned his grandfather had shared many stories of his service during the liberation of the Netherlands during WWII.

After a moment, I continued. One time my Daddy's curiosity got the best of him. He watched a Nazi soldier digging a fox hole at the edge of the bridge across from their property in anticipation of the rapidly advancing Canadian Army—Jeff's grandfather among them. The six-year-old boy mustered up all his courage and approached the soldier as he prepared his defences, "What are you doing?" Looking up, the soldier hissed at him, "I'm digging a hole to bury you in!" Terrified he ran and hid; not returning home until later that night. The next morning he found a large dead toad in the deserted fox hole; the memory haunted him for years. My dad recalls knowing they were liberated when one day, the German soldiers disappeared and the next day he saw Canadian Army trucks drive by. The Netherlands were officially liberated a few days later. The enduring bonds that tie our two countries together were cemented as thousands of cheering Dutch citizens, my family included, lined the streets; cheering, waving, and showing their gratitude as their liberators marched across their country. Canadian soldiers remained in Europe keeping the peace, rebuilding destroyed infrastructure, and burying thousands of their own. The Dutch donated a few properties that were designated Canadian cemeteries. The sacred and pristine grounds are visited every Christmas Eve as hundreds pay their respects by placing a candle at every grave of the brave men and women who gave the ultimate sacrifice for freedom. As part of the rebuilding, Canada offered to adopt orphans and open up immigration for thousands of Dutch families. Jeff's grandfather unsuccessfully tried to adopt a young orphan who reminded him of his own daughters waiting back in Canada. In the early 1950s, Oma and Opa packed up a few personal items and seized the opportunity to immigrate to Canada. Soon, Oma, Opa, and all but their eldest boarded a flight for Canada—excited for the opportunity to start a new life and honoured at the chance to become Canadian. Mesmerized by the views of the Canadian landscape outside the tiny window of their plane, Daddy talks about the flight and the following train ride in detail as if it happened yesterday. Leaving behind the only home they ever knew, in pursuit of the ultimate dream of freedom, opportunity, and becoming Canadian, as they offloaded in

Calgary, Alberta. Like my Daddy, I am a product of the amazing bond between our countries.

Immediately prior to leaving the old country, Oma and Opa bought the whole family new clothes; the finest "Sunday best" they could find, hoping to look affluent and blend into their new community. Daddy was grateful for the new clothes and he knew they were very expensive for his parents; yet he dreaded wearing his new ensemble. He quickly learned that what was fashionable in the old country caused him to standout in Canada. Daddy would sneak through the alley ways on his way to church to avoid the local kids for fear of being mocked. Looking at him, one would think he was a typical Canadian child with his blue eyes and blond hair. However, like many of the other Dutch kids, he was regularly teased and snickered at for his poor English, his Dutch clothes, and for being an immigrant. Because of his limited English, he was placed in grade seven despite having completed grade nine in the Netherlands. One afternoon at gym class he was sent to the principal's office for not having gym shoes. He explained that he only had one pair of shoes and his family could not afford gym shoes. I find it heartbreaking to imagine how devastated and embarrassed he must have felt at fifteen years old when the principal told him he was no longer welcome at school. He left, deflated and knowing the impact this unjust decision would have on his life. With his head held high he battled through discrimination as an immigrant through the years. Although discrimination towards him slowly faded away as he integrated into life in Canada and hid his heritage, the pain and lost opportunities always remained inside him.

* * *

Enjoying the beautiful blanket of stars from the deck of April Sun, I was starting to drift off to sleep, so we called it a night, slipped down below to our v-berth and snuggled in under our fluffy duvet. We drifted to sleep, cradled by the gentle rocking and ever so soothing sound of the ocean lapping against the hull as April Sun rested lazily on her anchor. It was truly magical and I found myself falling in love.

I awoke to gentle waves that had cradled and rocked us through the night. Jeff sat at the bedside happy to see me wake. He handed me a cup of freshly brewed vanilla coffee and his phone showing me a truly stunning photo of the morning sunrise moments before. Embracing me he whispered, "It was the most beautiful sunrise of the thousands I have seen . . . being here with you . . . " Wishing he had woken me to watch it with him, I admired the photo and sipped the delicious creamy coffee, enjoying the strong vanilla aroma. Shortly after our morning coffee and tasty breakfast wraps, we hoisted the anchor, waved good-bye to our neighbours, and motored away from our anchorage. Excited for the adventures the new day would bring, we enjoyed a gentle breeze and the crisp fresh smell of the ocean. We were both excited to set out on the water and finally set the sails for the first time! Once out of the lee of Albert Head, we found a perfect gentle breeze. Jeff turned off the engine and released the furler as I winched

in the jib sheet. In just a few minutes we were effortless-
ly gliding through the water. The simplicity, peacefulness,
and beauty was all I had imagined and more. The cool
gentle salty air danced over our sun-kissed skin and teased
my blonde hair. I felt so light, free, and at one with myself
and the world. Setting the autopilot, we laid on the foredeck and held hands. April Sun sailed past a few massive
herring balls that attracted hungry seagulls from above
and salmon from below. A large pod of porpoises elegantly dove through the water at our bow riding the waves like
a roller coaster—likely hunting the salmon.

We talked for hours about Jeff's adventures at sea and
why he had joined the Royal Canadian Navy. He talked
fondly about growing up with the utmost love, admiration,
and respect for his grandparents and how he spent his
childhood sailing and learning so much from them. He described his grandfather's position as the commanding officer of a photo reconnaissance unit overseas during WWII,
and his participation in the liberation of the Netherlands.
We agreed that his grandfather had likely marched past
my Daddy, the rest of my family, and all who lined the
streets celebrating their liberation so many years ago. As
our conversation continued, we were surprised how many
times our families and our own paths had crossed or nearly crossed, and how serendipitous it was to finally find
each other.

Having such a strong family history in becoming Canadian, I felt a calling greater than myself as an individual. After experiencing much adversity throughout my life,
I felt the need to do something good in the world and pro-

vide a safe secure future at home and afar for myself, my children, and every child. I felt a calling from my inner voice and my bones to serve my country. I wanted to be a part of the same military that had altered the course of my family's path; perhaps in my own small way to honour all those Canadians who had sacrificed their lives so long ago. Despite being a single mother with three young children, I was recruited on a Wednesday, swearing an oath of allegiance to Queen and country and signing a contract committing my life as collateral. The following days were a whirlwind. That Saturday I boarded a plane with a dear friend who had a similar calling. We shipped out to Quebec to complete our Basic Military Qualification (BMQ). Despite a training accident, which saw me severely injured, I did what every good soldier is trained to do and *soldiered on* through the debilitating pain and additional challenges my injury brought. My passion and determination came from thoughts of returning to my children, of new adventures that lay ahead, and of those who liberated Groningen and my family. The end of BMQ was bitter-sweet. Exhausted, in pain, and hugging my bestie goodbye prior to boarding the coach bus, we both headed to the airport bound for our respective postings: Canadian Forces Base (CFB) Esquimalt in Victoria, BC for myself; and CFB Ottawa for her—putting most of the country between us. I was now able to turn my focus on a much-needed surgery and rehabilitation to get myself ready to tackle a new career, Battle Fit training, upcoming career courses, and ultimately a deployment where I would have the opportunity to help others in need. I had been trained and had a successful career as a certified dental assistant prior to recruiting and I was eager to learn the military side of my profession. In crisp new fatigues, I quickly blended in, making new friends, learning the lingo, acronyms, and protocols. However, within days of arriving at CFB Esquimalt, my enthusiasm quickly evaporated. I was suddenly faced with severe harassment at the hands of my direct supervisor. It eventually became obvious that I was not alone as several co-workers experienced harassment, discrimination, and a very toxic work environment within the Dental Clinic at the Base Hospital. Between managing my injuries and the constant attacks from my supervisor, I truly felt helpless. I felt hopeful when I was temporarily posted from the Dental Detachment to the Joint Personnel Support Unit (JPSU) where service members could focus on medical rehabilitation—or so that was the intent when the military formed JPSU. However, it proved to be anything but a safe place for the injured to recover. While there, myself along with many others, were subjected to aggravated Military Sexual Trauma (MST), abuse of authority, threats, and extreme failures in leadership. What I had observed and personally experienced in only a few months was the complete antithesis of all that we were taught about the ethics and values of the Canadian Forces. Despite all the betrayal and failure of my leaders, I still held onto the ethos and ethics the Canadian Armed Forces were supposed to be about. Instead of suffering and *soldiering on* through the harassment and discrimination, I chose to take a stand. I started advocating, being a voice for others, speaking up to any and all that would listen, knowing full well that those who did speak up would soon lose their careers. Unwilling to experience or witness any more injustice and abuse, I choose to become the *sacrificial lamb*, so that I could affect real change. I stood up to my tormentors, bullies, and failed leaders. Ultimately this led to me being ostracised and forced into a medical release. I was heartbroken, confused, and felt betrayed, yet little did I realize at the time that I would still be able to serve my country in a way I would never have imagined.

Within a few months of our initial sailing adventure on April Sun, Jeff was appointed as the Captain of HMCS ORIOLE; which had been his dream since he joined the navy twenty-two years earlier. The historic tall ship is the oldest and longest serving ship in the Royal Canadian Navy. We discussed how we would manage with Jeff being required to be away at sea much of the year despite having just blended our young families and lives, all while dealing with my rapidly deteriorating health. We found the best balance as we could as I went from *Battle Fit*, *to unable to* work, and on a serious decline both physically and mentally. Now on long-term medical leave, I battled injuries turned permanent from continued medical mismanagement from the CAF. I quickly found myself spending most of my non-medically consumed time aboard HMCS ORIOLE with Jeff—the only place I felt safe on the base. Desperate to fulfill my oath to Queen and Country, I realized I could find fulfillment supporting Jeff's command and the ship's public relations mission. Our young family was blessed to be a part of many events through their formative years aboard HMCS ORIOLE and our somewhat dilapidated April Sun, learning about the ocean, sailing, family, and life skills. Jeff and I created a highly successful family-oriented platform for public relations and Junior Officer Training programs taking it to a level never seen before. The ship sailed the Pacific Northwest, engaging and connecting with hundreds of wonderful individuals, organizations, dignitaries, and foreign militaries all while training junior officers and sailors in teamwork, leadership, and seamanship. The kids and I often sailed with the ship or I would fly to ports of call to meet the ship and help with receptions, tours, charitable events, hosting dignitaries, and festivals. I recall vividly attending a reception onboard a United States Navy helicopter carrier during Seattle Fleet Week. As we approached the towering ship, I paused and gasped at the extensive five-story scaffolding stairs that led from the jetty up to the flight deck. I graciously thanked our driver as I wiggled my way out of the back of the town car in my cocktail dress, bracing myself between the door, balancing on one foot as Jeff pulled my crutches out and handed them to me. Lifting my non-complementary medical accessories, I gripped the padded handles with my hands, which were blistered and bleeding from years of using my crutches. Concerned the stairs were too daunting, Jeff kindly offered for us to skip the event and head back to the ORIOLE. I shook my head and slowly crutched to the base of the scaffolding where I was greeted by a young fit Marine. He stood wide-eyed. As we approached he saluted sharply and welcomed us. Looking at my crutches and cocktail dress, he gestured to another Marine and politely offered, "Ma'am, we will carry you up." Determined as ever, I confidently said, "Thank you, Sergeant, however I will carry myself up, I'm *Canadian Army Strong!*" Respectfully he nodded to me as he stepped aside and smiled, as I slowly conquered the stairs. During Jeff's five-year command, I created a new purpose in life for myself. It was a refuge from the harassment and discrimination that I experienced on the base and it allowed me to serve my country in a small way that rang true to the ethos I sought. Eventually, I was medically released from the military with severe and permanent disabilities leaving me in a very painful and dark place. Eventually, I was able to assemble an amazing medical and personal support system. Through resilience and sheer determination, I had found a new calling to serve a greater purpose for the betterment of myself, my family, and Canada. Soon I was on a new incredible journey, which I never could have imagined. I like to look at my experiences, both good and bad, and my disabilities as gifts which have allowed me to reach out in a different yet beautiful way. I am proud to be Canadian and enjoy the freedoms of this great nation, contributing to the greater good in my own small way with my pen and paper, connecting with other trauma survivors and like-minded people.

* * *

It seemed fitting that Jeff and I were married onboard HMCS ORIOLE where we served together and at Albert Head where we had our first sailing adventure together. In a way, it was symbolic of so many things: my Daddy, who had faced discrimination when he immigrated to Canada, walked me down the aisle to the ship where I was able to redefine and find a new life after the hardships and challenges of my life before ORIOLE, much like our family redefined their lives after leaving the Netherlands. To me, being Canadian is more than just being born here or having a Canadian passport. It is about contributing to the values and beliefs I sought in my career in the military. It is about giving of yourself to help and protect others much like the Canadian soldiers who sacrificed so much to liberate my family and the Netherlands.

Having the privilege of being born and raised in the safety of Canada has granted me many freedoms most in the world do not have. Despite the discrimination and unjust challenges my family faced initially as immigrants, we are grateful and proud of both our rich Dutch heritage and Canadian citizenship. With love and kindness we can come together as a nation and celebrate the great diversity of humankind ensuring equal opportunities and freedoms for all Canadians.

Acknowledgements

GBR would like to acknowledge the work of its authors. They, and we, have stood up against sexual abusers in places of authority—we have taken to the courts and media. We have fought for the best for our children in family court. We have sought justice for murdered BIPOC. We have spoken publicly on individual and business needs throughout the COVID-19 pandemic. We have united people within a culture and across cultures, and promoted women's rights in business, technology, the arts, medical, and armed forces. We have promoted medical rights, we have funded literacy programs for Indigenous Peoples in Canada and women of colour in third world countries, and so much more. We do the work where it needs to be done—to encourage harmony and growth.

-Ky-Lee Hanson
publisher at Golden Brick Road Publishing House

"To all the kind people that have been hurt. I speak with you, and I'll never stop. I wish you peace. Together we can shine on the darkness, and light the North in a way for the whole world to see."
-Ky-Lee Hanson

Acknowledgements

"I am eternally grateful to my parents for rising above the hardships and sacrifices they endured, to provide me with a better life. For granting me the opportunity to grow up in a country that has afforded me the rights and freedoms to become the strong woman that I am today. To all other immigrant parents, I commend you on your bravery and selflessness to ensure that your children have the opportunity to grow up in a better environment as free citizens."

-Nadia Dedic

"Thank you Ky-Lee Hanson for inviting me to be a part of Lighting the North. Thank you Sasha Ritchie for all your support through this journey. Thank you GBR Publishing Team."

-Shirin Ariff

"Immense gratitude and I raise my hands to the Tla'amin Nation for being miraculous hosts as you welcomed me and shared your culture with me. EMOTE!"

-Charleyne Oulton

"I dedicate these words to all missing and murdered Indigenous women and those affected by their disappearances. May they rest in peace and may their loved ones find comfort and closure. Chi miigwetch! (Thank you so much!)"

-Crystal Hardy Zongwe Binesikwe

Acknowledgements

"To the incredible lineage of strong women before me, including my grandmother Ella, and my mother Laura, for teaching me to stand up for myself and to believe in the power of love. And to my daughters Erin and Kyra, for being beautiful examples of the legacy of love I want to create and leave behind."

-Eldyka Simpson

"To my husband, Jonathan. Thank you for being a shoulder to cry on, the one that listens to my frustrations, the heart for loving me unconditionally, and the person for believing in me."

-Karen Swyszcz

"To my sisters, mother, and daughters. You push me, support me, and are helping to guide me to where I belong. My girls, I strive to make your future safe."

-Sasha Rose

"My utmost gratitude to those who have honourably served in uniform and to all those who have been light in my darkness when I was not able. Without you I wouldn't be."

-Angel Kibble

Check out some of our other titles

www.goldenbrickroad.pub

Shop at 20% off with promo code GOLD20

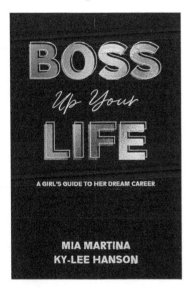

Check out some of our other titles

www.goldenbrickroad.pub

Shop at 20% off with promo code GOLD20

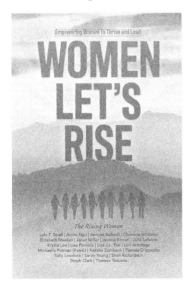

Check out some of our other titles

www.goldenbrickroad.pub

Shop at 20% off with promo code GOLD20

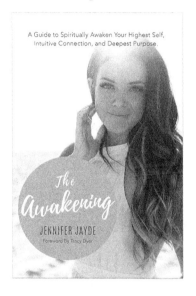

A Guide to Spiritually Awaken Your Highest Self, Intuitive Connection, and Deepest Purpose.

The
Awakening

JENNIFER JAYDE
Foreword By Tracy Dyer

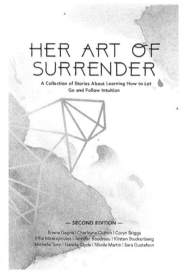

HER ART OF SURRENDER

A Collection of Stories About Learning How to Let Go and Follow Intuition

— SECOND EDITION —

Briana Gagné | Charleyne Oulton | Coryn Briggs
Effie Mitskopoulos | Jennifer Boudreau | Kirsten Stuckenberg
Michelle Tonn | Narelle Clyde | Nicole Martin | Sara Gustafson

Foreword by Catherine Reitman
Creator and Star of Workin' Moms

The
mama's
Gotta
Work!

Stories and Survival Hacks from Real-Life
Working Moms on Conscious Parenting,
Career Success, and True Fulfillment

Co-Authored By

Krysta Lee | Amanda Drexler | Andie Mack | Charleyne Oulton
Domenica Orlando | Elizabeth Meekes | Erin Montgomery
Laura Morris | Lisa Evans | Marcia Mietke | Mary Ann Masesar Blair
Melissa Killeleagh | Michelle Emmick | Nanci Lozano | Pina Crispo
Sally Lovelock | Sharlene Rochard | Sharon Hughes-Geekie
Stephanie Card | Teresa Nocita

Our world
is cool

Written by Linda Kovacs
Illustrated by Sarah Hankinson

GOLDEN BRICK ROAD
PUBLISHING HOUSE

Link arms with us as we pave new paths to a better and more expansive world.

Golden Brick Road Publishing House (GBRPH) is a small, independently initiated boutique press created to provide social-innovation entrepreneurs, experts, and leaders a space in which they can develop their writing skills and content to reach existing audiences as well as new readers.

Serving an ambitious catalogue of books by individual authors, GBRPH also boasts a unique co-author program that capitalizes on the concept of "many hands make light work." GBRPH works with our authors as partners. Thanks to the value, originality, and fresh ideas we provide our readers, GBRPH books have won ten awards and are now available in bookstores across North America.

We aim to develop content that effects positive social change while empowering and educating our members to help them strengthen themselves and the services they provide to their clients.

Iconoclastic, ambitious, and set to enable social innovation, GBRPH is helping our writers/partners make cultural change one book at a time.

Inquire today at www.goldenbrickroad.pub